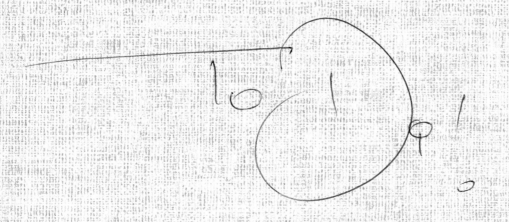

TURKISH MEZE

Enjoy My Delights!

Love
Sultan

TURKISH MEZE

Simple, delicious recipes for sharing

Sevtap Yüce

SBS

hardie grant books
MELBOURNE · LONDON

CONTENTS

INTRODUCTION

My mother went to school when she was seven. Her entire school — about fifty students — was taught in a single room. One section of the room was Class One, another section was Class Two, and so on. She didn't have writing paper or a book or a pencil. She broke her brother's pencil in half, then ripped off half his writing paper so she had some paper and a pencil to write with.

When she was sixteen, she met my father through an arranged marriage. They were married, and this was when my mother made her first meze. It was for my father.

In time her brother, Ibrahim Catma, became my father's best friend, and my favourite uncle. In those days meze was only for the men. They would sit at the table and the women would prepare the food. To start, they might nibble on a bowl of salted pistachios, or fresh green almonds and a little bowl of salt. They would dip the almonds into the salt and take a little bite, then have a sip of raki. The bottle of raki would sit in the centre of the table with a jug of water. Each man had two glasses in front of him. One glass would have two fingers of raki, the other glass would be full of water. The glass of raki would then be topped with fresh water, turning the clear raki cloudy, into what we called 'lion's milk'. As a child I was mesmerised watching the men turn two clear liquids into a cloudy nectar. Then they would raise their glasses and touch their hands together and say 'Can Cana' (pronounced 'Jan Jana'), meaning 'Life to Life'. If they were just friends they would say 'Serefe', meaning 'To your honour'.

Next the chunks of watermelon and feta would arrive, with slices of beautiful honeydew melon, crunchy fingers of cucumber, delicious deep-red tomatoes and tender, sweet green baby capsicums (bell peppers). After this would come the dishes of food braised in olive oil. A sip of raki, a sip of water, and morsels of the meze. Meanwhile the men would be chatting away solving the world's problems while the women prepared the next hot dish for the meze.

Nowadays we all sit together, men, women and children — all now share the same experience that our fathers and uncles and grandfathers shared. Now we are part of the whole experience, but you only make meze for your loved ones — those you wish to spend many, many hours with.

Meze is always a seasonal affair. Each region would have its own distinctive meze, depending on the local produce of each season. Winter would bring fresh glossy anchovies, tossed in flour, fried briefly and served with a chunk of juicy lemon. In spring, there'd be green beans, tomatoes and stuffed capsicums (bell peppers).

Music was always part of the experience. When I was a child, I watched the big black discs with a hole in the middle go round and round: vinyl records. If anyone could play an instrument, they would entertain us. Maybe someone would play the saz — a traditional long-handled stringed instrument.

Nowadays in Turkey you may go to a taverna or meyhane and the waiter will come to your table with trays of meze and you select the food your eyes are seduced by. Then you choose the main meal. Everything is shared, every little dish, and always there is much discussion about each morsel.

History tells us meze originated in Persia and spread throughout Turkey and beyond as the Ottoman Empire expanded. Today it is a way of living and eating, sharing all, including breakfast, lunch and dinner. For breakfast we drink tea, for lunch we drink ayran (a chilled yoghurt drink). As the sun goes down we drink raki or beer, or a glass of delicious wine. Times have changed!

There are no rules with meze. It is personal, it is seasonal, it is flexible — it is the food that matches your choice of drink. Also, it depends how much time you have in your busy life. The meze could be dishes such as stuffed vine leaves or zucchini (courgette), stuffed tomatoes, fried sardines or anchovies, or perhaps a purée of broad beans (fava beans), or an eggplant (aubergine) salad. There will be many small dishes to follow the meze.

My mother used to tell me a story about a sultan who had two sons. His favourite and elder son gave him all the gold and silver and treasures of the world, saying, 'I love you as much as all the treasures in the world.' The sultan replied, 'I love you, my son!' The sultan's younger son, however, told his father, 'I love you as much as all the grains of salt.' The younger son then prepared a huge meze table for his father, using no salt in any of the dishes. The sultan tasted the food and declared, 'Son, there is no flavour in this food!' To which his younger son replied, 'So, Father, now you know how I feel about you.'

This story taught me a lesson. I never put salt and pepper on my customers' tables with my meze: I believe food brought to the table should have all the love and seasoning in it already.

I came to Australia in 1985 as a child bride, at the age of sixteen, to marry the man arranged for me. Years went by and a woman called Elea became one of my most beautiful friends. One night I wanted to cook dinner for her. What could I make for my friend? It had to be the most delicious meal in the world, but at

the time I only had five dollars to spend. So I went to the greengrocer, then the supermarket, then the butcher. And then I went back to the vegie shop and bought some little bits of vegetables. Then I went back to the butcher and asked, 'Can I please get some chicken carcasses? How much will that be?' He said, 'Nothing for the chicken carcasses for you, little one.' So I went home, put the carcasses in the biggest pot I could find and fried them in a little oil until golden. I washed and chopped my vegetables and added them to my pot. I topped it up with a bit of water and salt and pepper and cooked it until my vegetables were tender. A few minutes later Elea arrived with a bottle of Australian chardonnay and I have never looked back! She still loves my soup.

When I was nineteen I met raki for the first time. It is the Turkish national drink, made with aniseed. For the first few mouthfuls we got on quite well. But after a few more mouthfuls we had a massive fight. You can imagine who won. (It wasn't me.) I didn't know how to drink like my father or my loved ones: I was a raki virgin! Raki and I haven't met since then. But, since every Turk thinks it is the lion's milk, it might be different for you…

More years passed, and by the age of twenty-seven I had my own restaurant in Angourie, a small coastal town in northern New South Wales. Times were tough, winters were quiet — so I began to arrange backgammon tournaments with meze platters for local families and new friends, and I was able to pay my bills.

Years later, I sit in my own home and think about my new Beachwood cafe, where people order everything off the menu, and how I carry out the sharing plates many times without even realising that I have created my own meze.

My meze has always been in my blood. It is the way I love to eat, the way I love to entertain, the way I love to share my food. When I look back at my life in Australia, all my cafes have been based on meze, but I have never written this on my menu blackboard. Today, I serve my meze plates to people and watch the smiles on their beautiful faces. When I clear the plates, they are empty, with finger swipes on them, and that makes me smile.

Now I want to share my meze with you.

DIPS

For me, dips are a delicious way of eating vegetables, blended with simple fresh ingredients. Dips can also be part of a main course, whether it is based around meat, poultry or seafood.

It is so easy to prepare your own dips instead of buying supermarket ones, which are often full of preservatives and high in calories. Making a dip can be as simple as roasting some beetroot (beet), grating it and folding it through garlic yoghurt. How happy your liver will be!

Notice the colours and textures of your dips. The different colours remind me of beautiful flowers.

CACIK
CUCUMBER YOGHURT

In summer, Turkish people thin this delicious dip with a little water and enjoy it as a refreshing cold soup with fresh crusty bread.

250 g (9 oz/1 cup) Yoghurt
(page 172)
2 garlic cloves, crushed
1 Lebanese (short) cucumber,
diced
30 g (1 oz/½ cup) chopped
dill
extra virgin olive oil, for
drizzling

In a bowl, gently mix together the yoghurt, garlic, cucumber and most of the dill. Season to taste with sea salt.

Drizzle with a little olive oil, garnish with the remaining dill and serve. This dip is best enjoyed straight away.

Serves 4

NANELİ YOGURT
MINT & GARLIC YOGHURT DIP

Please don't ever use bottled or pre-peeled garlic in your cooking. It is best if you peel your own garlic, whenever you use it, whether you crush it, fry it or chop it. Don't allow anyone else to handle your garlic, unless they are loved ones — otherwise the garlic can taste bitter or old, and you don't know where it comes from or who has fiddled with it!

If you are using large quantities of garlic, pop the cloves in warm water for a few hours and they will be much easier to peel.

250 g (9 oz/1 cup) Yoghurt
cheese (page 173)
2 garlic cloves, crushed
pinch of sea salt
25 g (1 oz/½ cup) chopped
mint, plus extra leaves to
garnish

Combine all the ingredients in a bowl. Garnish with extra mint leaves and serve with crusty hot bread.

This dip can be made several hours ahead and is wonderful with lamb or chicken.

Serves 4

AKDENIZ SALATASI

MEDITERRANEAN EGGPLANT & YOGHURT DIP

250 g (9 oz/1 cup) Yoghurt
   cheese (page 173)
5 garlic cloves, crushed
135 g (5 oz/½ cup) tahini
   (see note)
juice of ½ lemon
3 charred eggplants
   (aubergines) (page 169)
50 g (1¾ oz) walnuts,
   chopped
pul biber, for sprinkling
   (see note, page 22)

In a large bowl, gently mix together the yoghurt cheese, garlic, tahini and lemon juice.

Roughly chop the eggplants. Fold them through the yoghurt cheese mixture with the walnuts. Season to taste with sea salt and serve sprinkled with pul biber.

This dip can be made a day ahead.

Serves 4

NOTE

Popular throughout the Middle East, and widely available from health food stores, tahini is a paste made from toasted sesame seeds. Turkish tahini is often thinner than tahini from other countries. The oil from the sesame seeds tends to separate from the paste and settle on top, so simply stir the oil back into the tahini before using. For a heavenly breakfast, drizzle some tahini and honey over warm toasted Turkish bread.

SARIMSAKLI YOGURT

GARLIC YOGHURT

2 garlic cloves
1 tablespoon sea salt
500 g (1 lb 2 oz/2 cups)
   Yoghurt (page 172)

Crush the garlic cloves to a smooth paste using a mortar and pestle.

Gently fold the garlic and sea salt through the yoghurt; don't stir too vigorously as you don't want the yoghurt to liquefy.

Transfer to a clean bowl and serve.

This dip is wonderful with meat, chicken and vegetables, and will keep in the refrigerator for up to 5 days.

Makes about 500 g (1 lb 2 oz/2 cups)

DEREOTLU SALATALIK

CUCUMBER, DILL & YOGHURT DIP

30 g (1 oz/½ cup) finely
   chopped dill
50 g (1¾ oz/1 cup)
   chopped mint, plus extra
   leaves to garnish
1 garlic clove, crushed
1 Lebanese (short) cucumber,
   finely diced
250 g (9 oz/1 cup) Yoghurt
   cheese (page 173)
extra virgin olive oil, for
   drizzling

Mix together the dill, mint, garlic, cucumber and a pinch of sea salt. Gently fold the mixture through the yoghurt cheese.

Spread the dip on a flat plate. Drizzle with olive oil and garnish with some extra mint leaves.

Serve straight away, with Turkish bread.

Serves 4

CEVİZLİ PATLICAN

EGGPLANT & WALNUT DIP

The flavours of this dip will deepen if left to develop overnight, or for a day or two. It is especially delicious with lamb cutlets. Serve with warm Turkish bread, flatbread or good crusty bread.

1 charred eggplant
  (aubergine) (page 169)
2 garlic cloves, crushed
4 tablespoons finely chopped
  walnuts
60 ml (2 fl oz/¼ cup) extra
  virgin olive oil
250 g (9 oz/1 cup) Yoghurt
  cheese (page 173)
sweet paprika, for sprinkling

Roughly chop the eggplant and place in a bowl.

Mix together the garlic, walnuts and olive oil. Gently fold the mixture into the eggplant with the yoghurt cheese. Season to taste with sea salt.

Serve sprinkled with paprika.

Serves 4

PANCAR SALATASI VE ANTEP FISTIGI

ROASTED BEETROOT & PISTACHIO DIP

When roasting beetroot, it's a good to idea to bake a few extra to use in other recipes — and, of course, you'll save electricity if you roast them while something else is baking in the oven.

1 beetroot (beet), scrubbed but not peeled

250 g (9 oz/1 cup) Yoghurt cheese (page 173)

2 garlic cloves, crushed

2 tablespoons extra virgin olive oil, plus extra for drizzling

3 tablespoons pistachio nuts, crushed

Preheat the oven to 180°C (350°F).

Wrap the beetroot in foil. Place on a baking tray and roast for 45 minutes, or until just tender.

Leave the beetroot until cool enough to handle, then rub or peel the skin off. Finely grate the beetroot and fold it into the yoghurt cheese with the garlic and olive oil. Season with sea salt to taste.

Spread the dip on a flat plate. Drizzle with a little extra olive oil and sprinkle with the pistachios just before serving.

This dip can be made several hours ahead.

Serves 4

HAYDARI SALATASI

FETA & MINT DIP

250 g (9 oz/1 cup) Yoghurt
   cheese (page 173)
2 tablespoons chopped feta
3 garlic cloves, crushed
1 tablespoon dried mint
125 ml (4 fl oz/½ cup) extra
   virgin olive oil
1 tablespoon toasted cumin
   seeds, crushed (see note,
   page 44)
pinch of sea salt
1 tablespoon pul biber
   (see note)

Mix together all the ingredients, except the pul biber. Just before serving, sprinkle with the pul biber.

   This dip can be made a day ahead if time permits.

Serves 4

NOTE

Pul biber is a red powder made from dried Aleppo peppers.
It is mild to medium in heat and the Turkish love sprinkling it over just about anything. If you can't find it in spice shops or Middle Eastern grocers, you can use chilli flakes instead.

ANTEP EZMESİ

TOMATO DIP

This dip is incredibly delicious with any barbecued meat or chicken. Even more wonderfully, it can be prepared up to four or five days ahead, the flavours blending together and intensifying during that time … if you can wait that long!

1 onion
250 g (9 oz) vine-ripened
　　tomatoes
250 g (9 oz/1 cup) tomato
　　paste (concentrated purée)
30 g (1 oz/1 cup) chopped
　　flat-leaf (Italian) parsley
4 long green chillies,
　　chopped
125 ml (4 fl oz/½ cup)
　　lemon juice
125 ml (4 fl oz/½ cup)
　　extra virgin olive oil
2 teaspoons pul biber
　　(see note, page 22)

Grate the onion and tomatoes and place in a food processor.

Add the remaining ingredients and blend to a smooth paste. Season to taste with sea salt and freshly ground black pepper.

Transfer to a bowl, then cover and leave to rest for at least 2 hours before serving.

Serves 4

YOGURTLU NOHUT EZME

CHICKPEA, YOGHURT & TAHINI DIP

Lovely with meat and fish, this dip will develop in flavour if made a day or two ahead. When cooking chickpeas (garbanzo beans), adding ½ teaspoon bicarbonate of soda (baking soda) to the cooking liquid will help tenderise them. The actual cooking time will depend on the size and freshness of your chickpeas.

250 g (9 oz/1¼ cups) dried
  chickpeas (garbanzo beans)
2 tablespoons tahini
  (see note, page 16)
2 tablespoons Yoghurt
  (page 172)
juice of 1 lemon
3 garlic cloves, crushed
25 g (1 oz/½ cup) chopped
  mint
15 g (½ oz/½ cup) chopped
  flat-leaf (Italian) parsley
pul biber (see note, page 22),
  for sprinkling
2 tablespoons extra virgin
  olive oil

Soak the chickpeas overnight in plenty of cold water.

Rinse the chickpeas and place in a saucepan. Cover with fresh water and bring to the boil. Reduce the heat and simmer for 1–1½ hours, or until soft. Drain and rinse again.

Place the chickpeas in a food processor, along with the tahini, yoghurt, lemon juice and garlic. Season with sea salt and freshly ground black pepper and blend to a smooth paste. If the mixture is too thick, add a few drops of hot water.

Spread the dip onto a flat plate. Sprinkle with the mint, parsley and pul biber. Serve drizzled with the olive oil.

Serves 4

BAKLA EZMESİ

BROAD BEAN PURÉE

Broad (fava) beans are my favourite thing in the world. They are especially delicious in this dip, which keeps well in the refrigerator for up to 1 week.

350 g (12½ oz/2 cups) dried
   broad (fava) beans
125 ml (4 fl oz/½ cup) olive
   oil, plus extra for drizzling
2 onions, diced
6 garlic cloves, chopped
pinch of sugar
chopped dill, for sprinkling
sweet paprika, for sprinkling
lemon wedges, to serve

Soak the broad beans overnight in plenty of cold water.

Remove and discard the outer skins from the beans. Rinse the beans and set aside.

Heat the olive oil in a saucepan and gently fry the onion until golden.

Add the garlic, broad beans and 750 ml (25½ fl oz/3 cups) water. Simmer, uncovered, for about 45 minutes, until most of the liquid has been absorbed and the mixture becomes mushy, adding a little more water if necessary.

Place the mixture in a food processor with the sugar and blend to a smooth paste. Season to taste with sea salt and freshly ground black pepper.

Pour into an oiled mould or moulds (I use a small bread tin) and refrigerate overnight, allowing the mixture to set.

Turn the purée out onto a serving plate. Drizzle with a little extra olive oil, then sprinkle with dill and paprika.

Serve with lemon wedges, and Turkish bread of course.

Serves 4

MUHAMMARA

RED PEPPER DIP

Enjoyed throughout the Middle East, this classic dip is delicious with some Bulgarian feta spinkled over the top. It can be made up to a week ahead; the flavours will deepen.

2 tablespoons biber salcasi
  (see note)
125 g (4½ oz/1 cup)
  walnuts, roughly chopped
juice of ½ lemon
3 garlic cloves, crushed
2 tablespoons crushed dried
  red chillies
125 ml (4 fl oz/½ cup) extra
  virgin olive oil

Mix all the ingredients together in a bowl, then cover and refrigerate until needed.

Serve cold, with hot Turkish bread.

Serves 4

NOTE

Biber salcasi, or Turkish red pepper paste, is a thick, hot, spicy, dark red paste made from chilli peppers. You'll find it in Middle Eastern grocery stores.

SMALL DISHES

Small dishes are eaten after the dips. They hone your palate
and take your meze to the next level, and can be as simple as
folding pastry around a feta and parsley stuffing, or making
some little lamb kofte.

Sampling some small dishes such as these makes you ready
for the next excitement.

POGÇA

PARSLEY & FETA PIES

Turkish ladies love baking, and every Turkish lady has her own version of pogça. These delicious pies are so easy to prepare, and are fantastic for breakfast or lunch; you can also slip them into kids' lunchboxes, like my Mama used to do. They can also be frozen to keep on hand.

50 g (1¾ oz) butter, melted

125 ml (4 fl oz/½ cup) olive oil

60 g (2 oz/¼ cup) Yoghurt (page 172)

2 eggs, separated

450 g (1 lb/3 cups) plain (all-purpose) flour

1 tablespoon baking powder

150 g (5½ oz) feta, crumbled

15 g (½ oz/½ cup) finely chopped flat-leaf (Italian) parsley

1–2 tablespoons sesame seeds or nigella seeds (see note)

Preheat the oven to 180°C (350°F).

Mix the melted butter in a bowl with the olive oil, yoghurt and egg whites.

Add the flour, baking powder and a pinch of sea salt, then knead the mixture in the bowl until the dough feels like your earlobe. Cover the dough and let it rest at room temperature for 1 hour.

Mix together the feta and parsley and set aside.

Break off small pieces of the dough and roll them into walnut-sized balls. Using your fingertips, or a rolling pin, flatten them into 10 cm (4 inch) rounds, about 5 mm (¼ inch) thick.

Put about 2 tablespoons of the feta mixture in the middle of each round. Fold the dough into half-moons and pinch the edges together with your fingers.

Lightly stir the egg yolks with a fork, then brush over the pies to glaze them. Sprinkle with the sesame seeds or nigella seeds, or both if you must.

Bake for 20 minutes, or until the pastry is golden brown.

Serve hot, or cold — if you can resist them while they're hot!

Makes 20–25

NOTE

Nigella seeds look like tiny black sesame seeds. They have a unique aromatic flavour, and are often sprinkled over baked goods. You'll find them in spice shops.

BALIK KÖFTESI

FISH KOFTE

I love this dish because it is so simple and tastes so pure. You can use any fish you like, but this dish is best suited to oily fish, such as jewfish (mulloway), mackerel, mullet or sea bass.

2 large onions
1 kg (2 lb 3 oz) firm fish
    fillets, skin removed
2 tablespoons sumac
    (see note, page 48)
2 long red chillies, diced
15 g (½ oz/½ cup) chopped
    flat-leaf (Italian) parsley
500 ml (17 fl oz/2 cups)
    sunflower oil
lemon wedges, to serve

In a food processor, roughly chop the onions. Add the fish and pulse a few times. Add the sumac, chilli and parsley, season with sea salt and freshly ground black pepper, then process for a few more seconds — not too long, as you want the fish to stay a little bit chunky.

Transfer the mixture to a container and let it rest in the refrigerator for a couple of hours for the flavours to develop.

When you're ready to eat, heat half the oil in a large frying pan over medium–high heat.

When the oil is hot, break off bits of the fish mixture and roll into walnut-sized balls. Fry for 2 minutes on each side, or until just cooked through, adding more oil to the pan as needed.

Serve hot, with lemon wedges.

Serves 4

TUZLU BADEM

ROASTED ALMONDS

For a sweet version of these marvellous snacks, use icing (confectioners') sugar instead of salt. These are best enjoyed straight out of the oven, while they are still hot.

250 g (9 oz) raw unsalted almonds
1 tablespoon sea salt
1 egg white, lightly beaten

Preheat the oven to 180°C (350°F).

In a small bowl, mix together all the ingredients until well combined.

Spread the almonds on a baking tray and roast for 10 minutes. Tip into a small bowl and serve hot.

Serves 4

SIGARA BÖREGİ

CIGAR BOREK

These are absolutely wonderful for breakfast or lunch. Serve them hot, while the pastry is still crisp and the feta is all warm and oozy.

250 g (9 oz) feta
2 egg yolks
30 g (1 oz/1 cup) chopped
  flat-leaf (Italian) parsley
375 g (13 oz) packet filo
  pastry
sunflower oil, for pan-frying

In a bowl, mash the feta, egg yolks and parsley into a smooth paste. Season with sea salt and set aside.

Cut the filo pastry into 20 cm (8 inch) squares. Take two sheets of the cut pastry and stack them on top of each other; cover the rest with a damp cloth so they don't dry out.

Place 2 tablespoons of the feta mixture in the middle of the pastry stack. Fold two sides in, then roll up into a cigar shape, sealing the end closed with a dab of water.

Continue making more borek until all the ingredients are used.

Heat about 2.5 cm (1 inch) of oil in a saucepan or large heavy-based frying pan over high heat. When the oil is hot, fry the borek in batches for 4–5 minutes on each side, or until golden brown.

Drain briefly on paper towel and serve hot.

Makes about 12

PIRASA MÜCVERI

LEEK FRITTERS

Turkish cooks don't waste anything. When preparing the leeks, be sure to chop up a lot of the green leafy stem too, rather than using just the paler end near the root. Also, there is no need to peel the potatoes here, especially if using a thin-skinned variety, as the skin adds texture and locks in vitamins. Just ensure the potatoes are very clean before you grate them.

Before frying your fritters, make and cook up one small fritter and taste it, then adjust the seasoning if needed before cooking the rest. That way your guests will know you have cooked these fritters with love! They are best made just before serving, otherwise the eggs will make the vegetables a bit soggy. Try serving these fritters with crumbled feta or smoked salmon with a beautiful green salad, or as part of a yummy meze. You can also replace the plain flour with rice flour or polenta. Enjoy — they are delicious.

500 g (1 lb 2 oz) leeks, washed well and thinly sliced

15 g (½ oz/½ cup) chopped flat-leaf (Italian) parsley

50 g (1¾ oz/⅓ cup) plain (all-purpose) flour

2 small potatoes, grated

5 free-range eggs

125 ml (4 fl oz/½ cup) sunflower oil

Put the leek, parsley, flour and potato in a large bowl. Crack the eggs into the bowl, season with sea salt and freshly ground black pepper and mix together well.

Heat the oil in a heavy-based frying pan over high heat. When the oil is hot, spoon the leek mixture into the oil, into 5 cm (2 inch) rounds, and fry in batches for 3–4 minutes on each side, until golden brown.

Drain briefly on paper towel and serve warm.

Makes 15–20

PATATES KÖFTESİ

POTATO KOFTE

500 g (1 lb 2 oz) desiree or
    other all-purpose potatoes,
    scrubbed but not peeled
1 tablespoon cornflour
    (cornstarch)
100 g (3½ oz) cheddar
    cheese, grated
2 free-range eggs
30 g (1 oz/1 cup) chopped
    flat-leaf (Italian) parsley
200 g (7 oz/2 cups) dry
    breadcrumbs
sunflower oil, for pan-frying

Cook the potatoes in a saucepan of boiling water until tender —
about 20 minutes, depending on their size. Drain and leave until cool
enough to handle.

Peel the potatoes, then mash them in a large bowl. Add the cornflour,
cheese, eggs and parsley. Season to taste with sea salt and freshly ground
black pepper and mix well using your hands.

Take walnut-sized pieces of the mixture and shape them into pointed
kofte, like pointy eggs. Roll the kofte in the breadcrumbs.

Heat about 2.5 cm (1 inch) of oil in a large heavy-based frying
pan over high heat. When the oil is hot, fry the kofte in batches for
2–3 minutes on each side, until golden.

Drain on paper towel and serve warm.

Serves 4

MERCİMEK KÖFTESİ

LENTIL KOFTE

Crushed chillies or chilli flakes can be added to the kofte mixture, for those who enjoy a little spice in life. These kofte can be made three or four days ahead.

125 ml (4 fl oz/½ cup)
  olive oil
1 large onion, finely diced
2 tablespoons tomato paste
  (concentrated purée)
1 tablespoon cumin seeds,
  toasted and ground
  (see note)
250 g (9 oz/1 cup) red
  lentils
175 g (6 oz/1 cup) fine
  burghul (bulgur wheat)
30 g (1 oz/1 cup) finely
  chopped flat-leaf (Italian)
  parsley
lettuce leaves, to serve
lemon wedges, to serve

Heat the olive oil in a saucepan and gently fry the onion until golden.

Stir in the tomato paste, cumin, lentils and 750 ml (25½ fl oz/3 cups) water. Season with sea salt and freshly ground black pepper and bring to the boil, then reduce the heat and simmer for 10 minutes, or until the lentils are soft.

Stir in the burghul and parsley. Cook for a further 2–3 minutes, then remove from the heat and leave to rest for 30 minutes.

When cool enough to handle, roll the mixture into walnut-sized balls, using wet hands.

Serve warm or cold, on lettuce leaves, with lemon wedges on the side for squeezing over.

Serves 4

NOTE

Freshly toasted and ground cumin seeds add wonderful flavour to this simple dish. To toast cumin seeds, tip them into a small frying pan and lightly fry them over medium heat for a minute or two, until they smell fragrant, shaking the pan often to toss the seeds around so they don't burn. Then just grind them to a powder using a mortar and pestle (a fabulous kitchen tool — everyone should have one!), or a spice grinder.

ÇİG KÖFTE

SPICY RAW BEEF KOFTE

When I was a kid, my mother used to make this for the meze. She would knead it and knead it, but in the end it was always too spicy for us kids to eat! To save kneading time, you can soak the burghul in water for 10 minutes and then drain it well before mixing it by hand with the beef.

250 g (9 oz) lean minced (ground) beef
175 g (6 oz/1 cup) fine burghul (bulgur wheat)
1 onion, grated
3 spring onions (scallions), finely chopped
6 garlic cloves, crushed
2 tablespoons biber salcasi (see note, page 30)
2 tablespoons tomato paste (concentrated purée)
1 tablespoon sea salt
1 tablespoon chilli flakes
1 teaspoon ground cumin seeds
30 g (1 oz/1 cup) chopped flat-leaf (Italian) parsley
cos (romaine) lettuce leaves, to serve
lemon wedges, to serve

Put all the ingredients, except the lettuce and lemon wedges, in a bowl. Season with freshly ground black pepper, then mix together using your hands.

Now knead using your hands for 20 minutes, or until the burghul is softened by the fat from the beef, and your forehead begins to sweat (if you don't happen to have a good friend nearby to kindly wipe your brow)!

Shape the kofte into bite-sized pieces and place each one in the middle of a lettuce leaf. Squeeze the lemon wedges over and pop a kofte into your mouth. Yum yum.

Serves 4

PATATES YAVRULARI
POTATO BABIES

500 g (1 lb 2 oz) potatoes,
   scrubbed but not peeled
4 garlic cloves, crushed
2 tablespoons cumin seeds,
   toasted and ground
   (see note, page 44)
juice of 1 lemon
1 tablespoon dried mint
2 tablespoons extra virgin
   olive oil
2 tablespoons pul biber
   (see note, page 22)
1 tablespoon sumac
   (see note)

Cook the potatoes in a saucepan of boiling water until tender —
about 20 minutes, depending on their size. Drain and leave until cool
enough to handle.

Peel the potatoes, then grate the flesh into a large bowl. Add all
the remaining ingredients, except the sumac, and mix together until
well combined.

Take walnut-sized pieces of the mixture and form into small balls.
Roll the balls in the sumac and serve.

These delicious potato babies are best eaten the same day.

Serves 4

NOTE
Sumac is a tiny reddish-purple berry that grows throughout the Middle
East. The berries are dried, then crushed and added to dishes for a tangy,
lemony zing. Ground sumac is available from spice shops and Middle
Eastern grocery stores.

KADINBUDU KÖFTE

LADIES' THIGHS BEEF KOFTE

Turkish people love naming their dishes after ladies' body parts. We have a dish for the lady's fingers, one for the lady's lips, one for the lady's navel. This dish is named after the lady's thighs. Perhaps because they think ladies' thighs are yummy?

These kofte are delicious with the Tomato dip on page 27, or just on their own. The flavour will be even nicer if you can make them a day ahead.

100 g (3½ oz/½ cup)
   medium-grain white rice
20 g (¾ oz) butter
1 large onion, diced
500 g (1 lb 2 oz) minced
   (ground) beef
15 g (½ oz/½ cup) chopped
   flat-leaf (Italian) parsley
½ teaspoon ground allspice
½ teaspoon ground cumin
3 eggs
35 g (1¼ oz/¼ cup) plain
   (all-purpose) flour
sunflower oil, for pan-frying

Put the rice in a small saucepan with 250 ml (8½ fl oz/1 cup) water. Bring to the boil, reduce the heat, then cover and simmer for 10–15 minutes, or until the water has been absorbed and the rice is just tender. Set aside.

Melt the butter in a frying pan and gently sauté the onion for about 7 minutes, until golden.

Tip the onion into a large bowl. Add the rice, beef, parsley, allspice and cumin and season with sea salt and freshly ground black pepper. Add one of the eggs and mix well by hand. Cover and refrigerate for 30 minutes.

Wet your hands with cold water. Take a walnut-sized piece of the mixture and shape it into a torpedo-shaped 'thigh'. Continue shaping all the meat in the same manner.

Whisk the remaining two eggs in a bowl; put the flour on a plate. Roll each kofte in the flour, then dip it into the egg, allowing the excess to drip off, then roll again in the flour.

Heat about 2.5 cm (1 inch) of oil in a large heavy-based frying pan over high heat. When the oil is hot, fry the kofte in batches for 3–4 minutes on each side, until golden.

Drain on paper towel and serve hot or cold.

Serves 4

KUZU KÖFTESİ

LAMB KOFTE

These are simply to die for. They are especially wonderful with the garlicky minty yoghurt dips in the Dips chapter, and the Eggplant & walnut dip on page 18. The kofte will be even more flavoursome if you make the basic mixture a day ahead, then fry the kofte just before serving. They also cook up well on a barbecue.

250 g (9 oz) minced
  (ground) lamb
1 large onion, diced
30 g (1 oz/1 cup) chopped
  flat-leaf (Italian) parsley
2 tablespoons cumin seeds,
  toasted and ground
  (see note, page 44)
1 tablespoon ground allspice
sunflower oil, for pan-frying

Put all the ingredients, except the oil, in a bowl. Season with sea salt and freshly ground black pepper and mix together using your hands.

Cover and allow to rest in the refrigerator for at least 30 minutes.

Wet your hands and shape the mixture into walnut-sized balls.

Heat about 2.5 cm (1 inch) of oil in a large heavy-based frying pan over high heat. When the oil is hot, fry the kofte in batches for 2 minutes on each side, until golden brown.

Drain on paper towel and serve hot or cold.

Serves 4

DOLMAS

Turks love stuffing things: any leaf, any vegetable, any seafood.

These stuffed delicacies are what we call dolmas. You could use the same basic stuffing mixture with all these different ingredients, and the end result will always be unbelievable.

With each dolma, you taste the core ingredient — you may even taste a vegetable you thought you hated and end up adoring it!

Who would have thought you could take such a simple thing as a grape leaf, pop it into boiling water, refresh it in cold water, then fill it with a stuffing of rice and pine nuts or lamb, or even roll a grape leaf around beautiful, glistening sardines?

The world is your oyster. You can stuff just about anything and enjoy it.

ETLİ KABAK DOLMASI

STUFFED ZUCCHINI

I told you — Turks like stuffing everything, and here is just one example. If you wish, you can make this dish vegetarian by using more rice. I won't take any offence. Perhaps you think zucchini (courgettes) are boring old vegetables, but they are delicious this way.

When cooking the rice for the lamb stuffing, ensure it is still firm to the bite, as it will continue cooking in the stuffing. If you have any leftover stuffing, roll it into small balls and fry them until just cooked through.

3 zucchini (courgettes)

2 tomatoes, sliced

2 tablespoons olive oil

90 g (3¼ oz/⅓ cup) tomato
   paste (concentrated purée)

80 g (2¾ oz) butter, cut into
   small cubes

Garlic yoghurt (page 17),
   to serve

fresh herbs, such as mint, dill
   and parsley, to garnish

Lamb stuffing

200 g (7 oz) minced
   (ground) lamb

1 large onion, diced

15 g (½ oz/½ cup) chopped
   parsley

30 g (1 oz/½ cup) chopped
   dill

2 tablespoons dried mint

3 tomatoes, diced

2 tablespoons tomato paste
   (concentrated purée)

185 g (6½ oz/1 cup) cooked
   long-grain white rice
   (still al dente, not fluffy
   or tender)

Mix all the stuffing ingredients together in a large bowl. Season with sea salt and freshly ground black pepper and set aside.

Slice each zucchini into rounds about 5 cm (2 inches) thick. Using a small teaspoon, scoop out some of the inside flesh, without breaking the outer ring, and leaving enough on the bottom to hold the stuffing. Finely chop the scooped-out zucchini flesh and mix it through the lamb stuffing. Sprinkle sea salt inside each round of zucchini, then stuff each one firmly with the lamb mixture.

Pack the zucchini rounds in a saucepan large enough to hold them all in a single layer. Place a tomato slice on top of each round; you may need to cut the tomato slices into thirds or quarters if they are too big.

Mix together the olive oil, tomato paste and 250 ml (8½ fl oz/1 cup) water, then pour over the dolmas. Dot each one with butter.

Cover the pan and bring to the boil, then reduce the heat and simmer, covered, for 10–15 minutes, or until the zucchini is tender and the lamb stuffing is cooked.

Serve hot or at room temperature, drizzled with garlic yoghurt, and garnished with herbs.

Serves 4

BİBER DOLMASI

STUFFED BABY CAPSICUMS

Kim has been growing vegetables for about 15 years, and he still brings the cafe eggs, chillies, eggplants (aubergines) and fresh herbs. (And, being a bit of a hippy, Kim still doesn't wear any shoes!) He now also grows banana peppers, as well as baby green capsicums (bell peppers), which he harvests when they are only 5 cm (2 inches) long, still have thin flesh and a beautiful sweet flavour — just like the ones we used to have in the markets in Turkey.

I stuff Kim's baby green capsicums with rice and loads of other yummy things, braise them in a little olive oil and water, then serve them with lemon wedges, garlic yoghurt and, of course, warm Turkish bread.

1 kg (2 lb 3 oz) baby
   capsicums (bell peppers)
½ quantity Rice pilaf
   (page 171), cooked for an
   additional 10 minutes
1 tomato, sliced
125 ml (4 fl oz/½ cup)
   olive oil
1½ tablespoons sea salt
lemon wedges, to serve
Garlic yoghurt (page 17),
   to serve

Working with one capsicum at a time, push the stem down and, with a twisting and pulling motion, remove and discard all the seeds and membranes. Set aside.

Spoon the prepared pilaf into the capsicums, packing it in firmly. Use a slice of tomato to plug each capsicum opening to secure the filling. Place the capsicums in a saucepan large enough to hold them all in a single layer.

Mix the olive oil and salt with 500 ml (17 fl oz/2 cups) warm water, then pour the mixture over the capsicums. Cover the pan and bring to the boil. Reduce the heat and simmer, covered, for 15 minutes, or until the capsicums are tender and the filling is cooked.

Serve at room temperature, with lemon wedges and garlic yoghurt.

Once cooked, these will keep in the refrigerator for up to 1 week.

The capsicums can also be stuffed ahead of time and cooked just before serving, or prepared ahead, frozen and cooked as required. However, they do not freeze well once cooked.

Serves 4–6

PATLICAN DOLMASI

STUFFED EGGPLANT WITH TOMATO, ONION & GARLIC YOGHURT

This recipe is best made using long, slender eggplants (aubergines). You can stuff the eggplants ahead and cook them just before serving; once cooked, these delicious treats will keep in the refrigerator for up to a week.

250 ml (8½ fl oz/1 cup)
  olive oil
1 kg (2 lb 3 oz) Japanese
  eggplants (aubergines)
  (see note)
1 large onion, diced
500 g (1 lb 2 oz) tomatoes,
  finely diced
60 g (2 oz/½ cup) chopped
  green chillies
pinch of sugar
30 g (1 oz/1 cup) chopped
  flat-leaf (Italian) parsley
4 garlic cloves, slivered
Garlic yoghurt (page 17),
  to serve

Preheat the oven to 180°C (350°F).

Heat the olive oil in a large frying pan and fry the whole eggplants for 5–6 minutes over high heat, until soft, turning them regularly with tongs. Remove from the pan and set aside.

Add the onion to the pan and fry over medium heat, stirring until soft. Add the tomato, chilli, sugar and parsley. Season with sea salt and freshly ground black pepper and cook for 5 minutes.

Split the eggplants lengthways, keeping them intact along one side, then sprinkle the insides with sea salt. Poke the garlic into the flesh of the eggplants, then stuff them with the tomato mixture.

Place the eggplants on a baking tray. Add 250 ml (8½ fl oz/1 cup) water to the tray and cover with foil. Bake for 30 minutes, or until the necks of the eggplants are tender.

Enjoy warm or cold. Serve with the garlic yoghurt on the side for your loved ones.

Serves 4–6

NOTE

Eggplants (aubergines) are available in different shapes, colours and sizes. Instead of the large, egg-shaped, dark purple variety commonly used in Middle Eastern and Mediterranean cuisines, use the long, slender, dark purple ones (often known as Japanese eggplants) in this recipe, as they will cook through more quickly.

LAHANA DOLMASI

CABBAGE DOLMAS STUFFED WITH RICE & HERBS

This recipe uses the basic Rice pilaf stuffing from page 171. However, when preparing the stuffing, omit the pine nuts and currants and cook the pilaf mixture a little longer.

1 large white cabbage
1 quantity Rice pilaf (page
   171), prepared without the
   pine nuts and currants, and
   cooked for an additional
   10 minutes
60 g (2¼ oz/¼ cup) tomato
   paste (concentrated purée)
125 ml (4 fl oz/½ cup)
   olive oil
lemon wedges, to serve

Separate the cabbage leaves. Bring a large saucepan of water to the boil, and have a large bowl of cold water standing next to the stove.

Working in batches, drop the leaves into the boiling water for 3–4 minutes, until just soft. Drain the leaves, then pop them into the bowl of cold water to refresh them. Drain again.

Lay each leaf on a flat tray, with the core end facing you. Trim the hard core of the leaves, reserving the trimmings. Place some of the prepared pilaf in the centre, to suit the size of each leaf. Fold in the left and right sides and pull, rolling the leaf towards you like a cigar. Roll the remaining dolmas in the same way.

Put all the cabbage trimmings and scraps in a large saucepan, then place the cabbage rolls on top (it doesn't matter if they are in layers).

Mix together the tomato paste, olive oil, 250 ml (8½ fl oz/1 cup) water and a good pinch of sea salt, then pour the mixture over the rolls. Cover the pan and bring to the boil. Reduce the heat, cover and gently simmer for 30 minutes, or until the cabbage is tender and the filling is cooked.

Serve hot or cold, with lemon wedges.

Leftovers will keep in the refrigerator for 3–4 days, and can also be frozen.

Serves 4–6

KALAMAR DOLMASI

STUFFED SQUID

This recipe uses some of the basic Rice pilaf to stuff the squid. Prepare the pilaf as directed on page 171, adding 1 tablespoon ground allspice to the rice mixture; cook the rice until tender and leave the pilaf to cool before using it to stuff the squid.

The remaining pilaf can be used in other recipes, or frozen until required.

400 g (14 oz/2 cups) Rice pilaf (page 171), made with 1 tablespoon ground allspice and cooked until tender

2 kg (4½ lb) squid, cleaned (page 169)

125 ml (4 fl oz/½ cup) sunflower oil

lemon wedges, to serve

Taking a spoonful of the prepared pilaf at a time, and working with one squid at a time, spoon the stuffing into the squid and gently squeeze the filling down towards the other end. Continue spooning and squeezing more stuffing into the squid, until the filling almost reaches the top of the squid, taking care that the bottom end doesn't burst open. Secure the opening of each squid with a toothpick.

Heat the oil in a large heavy-based frying pan over medium–high heat. When the oil is hot, add the squid, in batches if necessary, and sprinkle with sea salt. Fry for 5–10 minutes, turning regularly, until each squid is just cooked.

If the squid are large, cut them into slices for serving, but if they are small, simply leave them whole.

Serve hot or at room temperature, with lemon wedges.

Serves 6–8

NOTE

The squid tentacles can also be used in the filling. Simply fry them in a little olive oil for about 2 minutes, then chop them up and stir them into the filling mixture.

If the squid is very fresh, it can be stuffed a day ahead and pan-fried just before eating.

PAZI DOLMASI

STUFFED SILVERBEET

1 kg (2 lb 3 oz) silverbeet
  (Swiss chard) leaves,
  weighed without stalks
1 quantity Rice pilaf
  (page 171), cooked for an
  additional 10 minutes
125 ml (4 fl oz/½ cup)
  olive oil
Cucumber yoghurt
  (page 14), to serve
lemon wedges, to serve

Preheat the oven to 180°C (350°F).

Pour 1 litre (34 fl oz/4 cups) water into a large saucepan and bring to the boil. Have a large bowl of cold water standing next to the stove.

Meanwhile, wash the silverbeet and trim off all the stems, so you end up with flat leaves. Pop the leaves in the boiling water for 2 minutes, then drain and immediately refresh in the bowl of cold water.

Spread the leaves out flat (there is no need to dry them first), with the wide part of the leaf closest to you. Place generous tablespoons of the pilaf at the base of each leaf. Working with one at a time, fold the left and right sides of each leaf into the middle, then roll slowly, pulling them in and making a firm cigar shape. Place the silverbeet rolls on a baking tray, snuggled alongside each other.

Mix the olive oil with 500 ml (17 fl oz/2 cups) warm water and season with sea salt and freshly ground black pepper. Pour the mixture over the silverbeet rolls. Cover with foil and bake for 20 minutes, or until the rice is tender.

Serve at room temperature, with lemon wedges.

Leftovers will keep in the refrigerator for 3–4 days; the rolls can also be shaped ahead and cooked just before serving.

Serves 4–6

MİDYE DOLMASI

STUFFED MUSSELS

In Istanbul, when walking over the Galata Bridge (or Galata Köprüsü as it is called in Turkish), you will see a lovely man, or woman, selling beautiful trays of stuffed mussels with a little wedge of lemon on the side. The mussels are truly amazing and everyone should experience them in Istanbul. You prise the shell open, squeeze a little lemon juice in, pop the mussel in your mouth, then give the empty shell back. You are in heaven! Here is how you can enjoy this experience at home.

1 kg (2 lb 3 oz) black mussels
40 g (1½ oz/¼ cup) pine nuts
2 large onions, finely diced
300 ml (10½ fl oz) olive oil
220 g (8 oz/1 cup) medium-grain white rice
1 ripe tomato, diced
15 g (½ oz/½ cup) chopped flat-leaf (Italian) parsley
pinch of sugar
35 g (1¼ oz/¼ cup) currants
1 tablespoon ground allspice
60 ml (2 fl oz/¼ cup) lemon juice
lemon wedges, to serve

Scrub the mussels and remove the hairy beards. Rinse the mussels in cold water, then place in a strainer and set aside.

Place the pine nuts in a large heavy-based saucepan and stir constantly over medium heat for a few minutes, until golden brown. Add the onion and 150 ml (5 fl oz) of the olive oil and slowly fry until the onion is soft and golden.

Stir in the rice, tomato, parsley, sugar, currants, allspice and lemon juice. Add 125 ml (4 fl oz/½ cup) water, season with sea salt and freshly ground black pepper, then cover and cook over low heat for 10–15 minutes, or until the rice is just cooked. Remove from the heat and allow to cool.

Meanwhile, add 3 tablespoons sea salt to a large bowl of water. Add the mussels and leave to sit for 5 minutes, until they open slightly. Gently prise them open with a spoon, without breaking the hinge.

Using a small spoon, stuff each mussel with some of the rice mixture, then close them back up again.

Place the mussels in the same saucepan the onion was cooked in. Pour in 250 ml (8½ fl oz/1 cup) water and the remaining 150 ml (5 fl oz) olive oil. Cover the mussels with a large heatproof ceramic plate, to weigh them down. Cover the pan with a lid and simmer the mussels for 10 minutes, or until just cooked. (Test by taking one out; the rice should be tender and the mussel sweet and juicy.)

Serve at room temperature, or chilled, with lemon wedges for squeezing over.

Serves 4

KARNIYARIK

'SPLIT BELLY' (STUFFED EGGPLANT WITH LAMB OR BEEF)

This is everyone's favourite in Turkey. I know it is another eggplant (aubergine) dish, but it is simply exquisite. Long, slender purple eggplants are ideal for this recipe, if you can get them — just leave them whole for the pan-frying step, rather than cutting them in half. Here I've used the round chubby ones; make sure yours don't have seeds in them, as these can make the flesh taste bitter.

You can also make this dish using boneless, skinless chicken thighs instead of the lamb or beef.

4 eggplants (aubergines)
  (see note, page 60)
125 ml (4 fl oz/½ cup)
  olive oil
2 onions, finely diced
2 small green capsicums
  (bell peppers), finely diced
300 g (10½ oz) minced
  (ground) lamb or beef
500 g (1 lb 2 oz) tomatoes,
  finely diced, plus 6 slices
  ripe tomato
2 tablespoons tomato paste
  (concentrated purée)
15 g (½ oz/½ cup) chopped
  flat-leaf (Italian) parsley
4 garlic cloves, sliced
Garlic yoghurt (page 17),
  to serve

Preheat the oven to 180°C (350°F).

Using a small knife, peel each eggplant lengthways, in striped-pyjama fashion. Cut each one in half and set aside.

Heat the olive oil in a large frying pan and fry the eggplants over high heat for 5 minutes, until evenly browned all over, turning them regularly with tongs. Remove from the pan and set aside.

Add the onion to the pan and fry over medium heat, stirring until soft. Add the capsicum and cook for 2 minutes.

Add the lamb or beef, diced tomato, tomato paste and most of the parsley, reserving some for garnishing. Season with sea salt and freshly ground black pepper and cook for a further 5 minutes. (The meat will continue cooking in the oven, so it doesn't need to be fully cooked at this stage.)

Place the eggplants on a baking tray, cut side up. Gently open the bellies, then sprinkle the insides with sea salt. Poke the garlic slices into the eggplant flesh. Spoon the meat filling into the belly of each eggplant, then cover each with a slice of tomato.

Pour 125 ml (4 fl oz/½ cup) hot water over the eggplants, cover with foil and bake for 45 minutes, or until the necks of the eggplants are tender.

Garnish with the reserved parsley and serve hot, with garlic yoghurt, a green salad and Turkish bread.

Serves 6

SALADS

Turks adore their salads. They love salads for breakfast, which
might be a chopped boiled egg tossed with some flat-leaf (Italian)
parsley, spring onion (scallion) and salt and pepper. For lunch they
might enjoy tomatoes, cucumbers and red onion, chopped into small
bite-sized pieces and dressed with parsley, lemon juice and olive oil.
Dinner salads might feature finely chopped carrots, radishes, lettuce
leaves, tomatoes and green chillies — whatever
is fresh and in season.

Packed with a whole range of flavours, salads are surely one
of the healthiest ways to enjoy the abundance Mother Nature
offers from season to season.

MERCİMEK SALATASI

WARM LENTIL SALAD

2 beetroot (beets), scrubbed
  but not peeled
300 g (10½ oz/2 cups)
  butternut pumpkin
  (squash), peeled and cut
  into 1 cm (½ inch) cubes
185 g (6½ oz/1 cup) brown
  lentils
60 g (2 oz/½ cup) Dukkah
  (page 170)
1 red chilli, diced
½ red onion, thinly sliced
20 g (¾ oz/1 cup) mint
  leaves
60 ml (2 fl oz/¼ cup)
  pomegranate molasses
  (see note)
125 ml (4 fl oz/½ cup)
  olive oil

Preheat the oven to 180°C (350°F).

Individually wrap each beetroot in foil. Place on a non-stick baking tray with the pumpkin and roast for 45 minutes, or until just tender. Remove from the oven and leave until cool enough to handle.

Meanwhile, rinse the lentils and place in a saucepan with 750 ml (25½ fl oz/3 cups) water. Bring to the boil, then reduce the heat and simmer rapidly for 35 minutes, or until just tender. Drain the lentils and place in a large bowl.

Rub or peel the skin off the cooled beetroot. Cut the beetroot into wedges or cubes and add to the lentils with the remaining ingredients. Gently mix together.

Serve warm, or at room temperature.

Serves 4

NOTE

Pomegranate molasses is made from the dark red juice of the pomegranate fruit, which has been cooked down to form a thick, tangy syrup. It is available from Middle Eastern grocers and fine food stores.

ENGINARLI PATATES SALATASI

ARTICHOKE & POTATO SALAD

7 artichoke hearts (page 168)
1 teaspoon plain
  (all-purpose) flour
juice of 2 lemons
3 potatoes, scrubbed but
  not peeled
80 ml (2½ fl oz/⅓ cup)
  olive oil
3 tablespoons chopped
  flat-leaf (Italian) parsley

Put the artichoke hearts in a saucepan with the flour, half the lemon juice, a good pinch of sea salt and 500 ml (17 fl oz/2 cups) water. Bring to the boil, then reduce the heat to medium and cook, uncovered, for 20 minutes, or until the artichoke hearts are tender. Remove from the heat and set aside to cool for 10 minutes.

In a separate saucepan, boil the potatoes for 20 minutes, or until just tender. Drain and allow to cool.

Peel the potatoes and place in a bowl. Mash them roughly with the olive oil, remaining lemon juice, most of the parsley, reserving some to garnish, and sea salt to taste.

Arrange the artichoke hearts on a plate and fill them with the potato mixture. Serve at room temperature, garnished with the reserved parsley.

This salad is best enjoyed straight away.

Serves 7

GAVURDAGI SALATASI

FOREIGN LAND SALAD

When Turkish people leave their mother country to make a new life abroad, this is the salad that always reminds them of home.

3 vine-ripened tomatoes

2 tablespoons pomegranate molasses (see note, page 72)

1 red onion, diced

20 g (¾ oz/1 cup) mint leaves

30 g (1 oz/1 cup) chopped flat-leaf (Italian) parsley

2 long green chillies, finely chopped

50 g (1¾ oz) walnuts, finely chopped

250 ml (8½ fl oz/1 cup) extra virgin olive oil

pul biber (see note, page 22), for sprinkling

Cut the tomatoes into 1 cm (½ inch) cubes and set aside.

In a serving bowl, mix together the remaining ingredients, except the pul biber. Season with sea salt and freshly ground black pepper, then gently mix the tomatoes through.

Serve at room temperature, sprinkled with pul biber.

This salad is best enjoyed soon after making.

Serves 4

SEMİZOTU SALATASI

PURSLANE SALAD

Purslane is the world's quickest, healthiest and easiest food. You will love it forever. It is full of goodness, and it is delicious. Purslane is also known as pigweed in Australia, yet it is the most wonderful vegetable. Many of us probably have it in our gardens and we pull it out as if it were a noxious weed. Please don't do this. Instead, harvest it and cook it and you will be sure to impress everyone.

2 garlic cloves, crushed
250 g (9 oz/1 cup) Yoghurt
   cheese (page 173)
250 g (9 oz) purslane
extra virgin olive oil, for
   drizzling

Fold the garlic through the yoghurt cheese.
   Wash the purslane and discard the thick stalks. Separate any larger leaves.
Mix the purslane through the yoghurt cheese and season with sea salt.
   Arrange the salad on a flat plate, drizzle with olive oil and serve.
   This salad can be prepared several hours ahead.

Serves 4

SOGANLI MAYDANOZ

PARSLEY & RED ONION SALAD

This simple salad is delicious with Turkish pizzas, and also barbecued chicken, lamb or beef.

15 g (½ oz/½ cup) chopped
   flat-leaf (Italian) parsley
1 red onion, thinly sliced
2 tablespoons sumac
   (see note, page 48)

Pile the parsley, onion and sumac on a chopping board. Sprinkle
with a pinch of sea salt, then rub the ingredients together.
   Place in a bowl and serve.
   This salad is best served straight away.

Serves 4

BEYİN SALATASI

BRAIN SALAD

2 lamb's brains, weighing
　about 100 g (3½ oz) each
125 ml (4 fl oz/½ cup)
　white vinegar
2 vine-ripened tomatoes,
　diced
1 red onion, thinly sliced
juice of 1 lemon
1 tablespoon sumac
　(see note, page 48)
1 tablespoon dried mint
60 ml (2 fl oz/¼ cup)
　olive oil

Soak the brains in a bowl of salted water for about 1 hour.

Drain the soaked brains, then place them in a saucepan with the vinegar and 500 ml (17 fl oz/2 cups) water. Bring to a simmer and poach gently for 15 minutes, until the brains are just cooked — they will be soft when you poke them with a sharp knife.

Remove the brains from the liquid and leave for 10 minutes, until cool enough to handle. Carefully remove all the membranes, peeling them off with your fingers. Set the brains aside and allow to rest at room temperature.

Place the tomato and onion in a serving bowl. Add the lemon juice, sumac, mint and olive oil and mix together. Season to taste with sea salt.

Slice the brains thinly and add to the salad. Serve at room temperature.

Serves 4

İLKBAHAR SALATASI

SPRING SALAD

1 baby cos (romaine) lettuce
2 vine-ripened tomatoes
1 Lebanese (short) cucumber
6 red radishes
2 spring onions (scallions)
125 ml (4 fl oz/½ cup) extra
  virgin olive oil
60 ml (2 fl oz/¼ cup) red
  wine vinegar
75 g (2¾ oz/½ cup)
  crumbled goat's cheese
10 g (¼ oz/½ cup) mint
  leaves
10 black olives, ideally
  kalamata

Separate the lettuce leaves, then wash and drain well. Roughly shred the lettuce and place in a serving bowl.

Roughly chop the tomatoes. Slice the cucumber into thin rounds, cut the radishes into thin wedges and finely slice the spring onions. Add the vegetables to the lettuce and gently toss.

Whisk the olive oil and vinegar with a sprinkle of sea salt and freshly ground black pepper, then drizzle over the salad.

Arrange the goat's cheese, mint leaves and olives on top and serve straight away.

Serves 4

NOHUT SALATASI

CHICKPEA SALAD

8 spring onions (scallions)

165 g (6 oz/1 cup) cooked
or tinned chickpeas
(garbanzo beans)

1 vine-ripened tomato, diced

60 ml (2 fl oz/¼ cup) apple
cider vinegar

16 green olives, pitted and
chopped

10 g (¼ oz/½ cup) mint
leaves

15 g (½ oz/½ cup) chopped
flat-leaf (Italian) parsley

125 ml (4 fl oz/½ cup) extra
virgin olive oil

Cut off the spring onion roots and just the very tops of the dark green stems. (Turkish cooks waste as little as possible!) Now chop the spring onions, including the green stems, and place in a bowl.

Add the remaining ingredients, along with a good sprinkling of freshly ground black pepper. Gently mix together.

Serve straight away, at room temperature.

Serves 4

KIRMIZI LAHANA SALATASI

RED CABBAGE SALAD

This salad can be made a few hours ahead and is a wonderful accompaniment to barbecued dishes.

1 baby red cabbage
2 tablespoons apple cider
   vinegar
2 garlic cloves, crushed
125 ml (4 fl oz/½ cup) extra
   virgin olive oil
1 carrot, grated
60 g (2¼ oz/¼ cup) good-
   quality mayonnaise
15 g (½ oz/½ cup) chopped
   flat-leaf (Italian) parsley

Remove and discard the outer leaves of the cabbage. Very thinly slice the cabbage and place in a large bowl.

Add the vinegar, garlic, olive oil and a good pinch of sea salt. Toss together, then cover and set aside for 15 minutes.

Add the carrot and mayonnaise and fold together. Serve sprinkled with the parsley.

Serves 4

PANCAR SALATASI

BEETROOT SALAD WITH ARTICHOKES

Turkish artichokes are really large, so you may need to alter the quantities of the beetroot (beet) mixture. Any leftover beetroot mixture can be turned into a delicious dip by adding some Garlic yoghurt (page 17) and Dukkah (page 170).

6 artichoke hearts (page 168)

juice of 2 lemons

3 beetroot (beets), scrubbed
  but not peeled

60 ml (2 fl oz/¼ cup)
  red wine vinegar

3 garlic cloves, crushed

1 carrot

250 ml (8½ fl oz/1 cup)
  extra virgin olive oil

1 vine-ripened tomato, diced
  (optional)

Place the artichoke hearts in a large saucepan with half the lemon juice and plenty of water. Bring to the boil, then reduce the heat to medium and cook, uncovered, for 20 minutes, or until the artichoke hearts are tender. Remove from the heat and set aside to cool for 10 minutes.

Meanwhile, place the beetroot in a separate saucepan with 250 ml (8½ fl oz/1 cup) water. Bring to the boil, then cover and cook for 30 minutes, or until just tender. Drain and leave to cool slightly.

Rub or peel the skin off the beetroot, then roughly grate the flesh into a bowl. Stir the vinegar and garlic through. Set the mixture aside until the artichokes are ready.

Grate the carrot and add to the beetroot with the remaining lemon juice and the olive oil. Season to taste with sea salt and freshly ground black pepper.

Arrange the artichoke hearts on a plate. Fill them with the beetroot mixture, then top with some diced tomato if desired.

Serve at room temperature. This salad can be made several hours ahead.

Serves 6

VEGETABLES

In Turkey, vegetables are eaten in abundance, varying with the season.

In summer, we enjoy shiny purple eggplants (aubergines),
the sweetest red tomatoes, the most beautiful pale green capsicums
(bell peppers) and tiny little baby cucumbers. Each season has
amazing vegetables to offer.

You can fry them. You can stuff them. You can braise them.
Just love them.

PATLICAN KIZARTMASI

FRIED EGGPLANTS WITH CHILLIES & GARLIC YOGHURT

Serve this dish at room temperature with warm crusty bread, ideally Turkish bread. It can be served as part of the meze, as a starter, or as a main meal. You can use either small fresh green chillies or the pale green banana chillies in this recipe, depending on how hot you like things.

2 eggplants (aubergines)
100 g (3½ oz) fresh
  green chillies
sunflower oil, for pan-frying
4 vine-ripened tomatoes,
  diced
Garlic yoghurt (page 17),
  to serve

Slice the eggplants into discs about 1 cm (½ inch) thick. Wash and dry the chillies. If using small chillies, leave them whole; if using banana chillies, remove the seeds and membranes.

Heat about 2.5 cm (1 inch) of oil in a large heavy-based frying pan. When the oil is hot, fry the eggplant discs in small batches over high heat for 2–3 minutes on each side, or until soft and browned. Remove each batch with a slotted spoon and drain on paper towel.

Add the chillies to the hot oil and fry, turning them constantly, for 5–10 minutes, or until browned all over. Remove with a slotted spoon and drain on paper towel.

Pour the oil into a heatproof container to reuse in other recipes.

Put the tomatoes in the hot pan and sprinkle with sea salt. Braise over low heat for about 5 minutes, until soft and juicy.

Arrange the eggplant discs on a serving plate. Top with the chillies and braised tomatoes. Serve with garlic yoghurt for spooning over.

Serves 4

ZEYTINYAGLI ENGİNAR VE BEZELYE

ARTICHOKES BRAISED IN OLIVE OIL WITH PEAS

Here is yet another yummy artichoke recipe. This one is divine. If you can't get hold of fresh peas, you can use frozen peas or fresh or frozen broad beans (fava beans) in this dish.

If using fresh broad beans, remove them from their big green pods, then freeze them for 20 minutes — the outer skins will slip off more easily. This method also retains more nutrients than boiling the skins off the beans.

125 ml (4 fl oz/½ cup) extra
  virgin olive oil
2 carrots, diced
500 g (1 lb 2 oz) artichoke
  hearts (page 168)
2 potatoes, peeled and diced
2 garlic cloves, finely
  chopped
1 tablespoon sugar
200 g (7 oz/1⅓ cups)
  podded fresh peas
370 g (13 oz/2 cups)
  double-peeled broad
  (fava) beans
30 g (1 oz/½ cup) chopped
  dill

Heat the olive oil in a large, wide, heavy-based saucepan. Add the carrot and fry over medium–high heat for 5 minutes.

Add 250 ml (8½ fl oz/1 cup) water, the artichoke hearts, potato, garlic and sugar. Season with sea salt and freshly ground black pepper. Bring to the boil, then reduce the heat to low and cook, uncovered, for 10 minutes.

Add the peas and broad beans and cook for a further 5 minutes.

Just before serving, stir in most of the dill, leaving some to garnish. Serve at room temperature, or chilled.

This dish can be made several days ahead.

Serves 4

SAKSUKA

EGGS IN FRIED EGGPLANT WITH TOMATO & GREEN CHILLI

100 g (3½ oz) long mild
  green chillies
2 eggplants (aubergines)
250 ml (8½ fl oz/1 cup)
  olive oil
500 g (1 lb 2 oz) tomatoes,
  peeled and diced
2 free-range eggs

Chop the chillies into small pieces. Cut the eggplants into 1 cm (½ inch) cubes.

Heat the olive oil in a large heavy-based frying pan. Add the chilli and fry over high heat for about 5 minutes.

Season with sea salt and freshly ground black pepper, then stir in the eggplant and cook for 10 minutes, or until the eggplant is soft.

Add the tomato and cook for a further 10 minutes to reduce and slightly thicken the mixture.

Using a spoon, make a little hollow in the tomato mixture for each egg. Break the eggs into the hollows. Cover and cook for 2 minutes, or until the egg whites have set but the yolks are still soft.

Serve hot, with Turkish bread.

Serves 2

ZEYTINYAGLI PIRASA

BRAISED BABY LEEKS WITH LEMON

1 kg (2 lb 3 oz) baby leeks
250 ml (8½ fl oz/1 cup)
  extra virgin olive oil
juice of 1 lemon
1 tomato, diced
1 tablespoon caster
  (superfine) sugar

Preheat the oven to 200°C (400°F).

Trim the roots from the leeks, and just a little bit off the very top of the green leafy stems.

Wash the leeks well and lay them on a non-stick baking tray large enough to hold them all in a single layer.

Mix together the remaining ingredients and pour over the leeks. Season lightly with sea salt and freshly ground black pepper, then cover with foil and bake for 30 minutes, or until the leeks are just tender.

The leeks can be braised 3–4 days ahead, but are best served at room temperature.

Serves 4–6

YUMURTALI PAZI

SILVERBEET WITH EGGS

500 g (1 lb 2 oz) silverbeet
(Swiss chard) leaves, washed
well, stems removed
40 g (1½ oz) butter
1 tablespoon olive oil, plus
extra for drizzling
1 onion, diced
4 free-range eggs
2 garlic cloves, crushed
250 g (9 oz/1 cup) Yoghurt
(page 172)
sweet paprika, for sprinkling

Bring about 2 litres (70 fl oz/8 cups) water to the boil in a saucepan. Plunge the silverbeet leaves into the boiling water and blanch for 2–3 minutes. Drain well, leave to cool, then squeeze the excess water away. Set aside.

Heat the butter and oil in a frying pan. Fry the onion over medium heat for 5 minutes, until soft and golden.

Thinly slice the silverbeet and add to the pan. Cook, stirring, for a few minutes, until the silverbeet is soft. Season with sea salt and freshly ground black pepper.

Using a spoon, make a little hollow in the silverbeet mixture for each egg. Break the eggs into the hollows. Cover and cook for 2 minutes, or until the egg whites have set but the yolks are still soft.

Meanwhile, using a mortar and pestle, crush the garlic with a pinch of sea salt. Fold the mixture into the yoghurt.

Pour the yoghurt mixture over the eggs. Drizzle with a little extra olive oil, sprinkle with paprika and freshly ground black pepper and serve.

Serves 4

ZEYTINYAGLI ENGINAR

ARTICHOKES BRAISED IN OLIVE OIL

Artichokes are best friends with your liver. It is a good idea to have plenty in your meze — so you can drink more. This is one of my favourite dishes.

By the way, don't pour the poaching water from the artichokes down the drain. It actually tastes nice and healthy and is excellent for flushing the liver and kidneys.

4 artichoke hearts (page 168)
8 spring onions (scallions),
  roughly chopped
juice of ½ lemon
pinch of sugar
125 ml (4 fl oz/½ cup)
  olive oil
chopped dill, to garnish
lemon wedges, to serve

Put the artichoke hearts in a saucepan. Add the spring onion, lemon juice and sugar. Stir in the olive oil and 125 ml (4 fl oz/½ cup) hot water and add a good pinch of sea salt.

Bring to the boil, then reduce the heat to medium and cook, uncovered, for 20 minutes, or until the artichokes are tender. Remove from the heat and set aside to cool for 10 minutes, then drain.

Serve the artichoke hearts at room temperature, garnished with dill, and with lemon wedges for squeezing over.

The artichokes can be prepared several hours ahead.

Serves 4

BARBUNYA PİLAKİSİ

BRAISED BORLOTTI BEANS

With their striking white, pink and purple colouring, fresh borlotti (cranberry) beans are surely one of the most beautiful things in the world. Their season is very short, so do make the most of them whenever you come across them. Here's a wonderful way to enjoy them.

1 kg (2 lb 3 oz) fresh
    borlotti (cranberry) beans,
    podded (see note)
250 ml (8½ fl oz/1 cup)
    olive oil
2 onions, diced
2 carrots, chopped
250 g (9 oz) tomatoes, diced
1 tablespoon sugar
juice of 1 lemon
15 g (½ oz/½ cup) chopped
    flat-leaf (Italian) parsley

Bring 750 ml (25½ fl oz/3 cups) water to the boil in a saucepan. Add the beans and boil for 15 minutes. Drain and set aside.

Wipe out the saucepan and add the olive oil. Fry the onion over medium heat for 5–10 minutes, or until golden and soft.

Add the beans, carrot and tomato. Stir in the sugar and season with sea salt and freshly ground black pepper. Pour in 250 ml (8½ fl oz/1 cup) water and bring to the boil, then reduce the heat to a simmer. Cover and cook for 45 minutes, or until the beans are soft.

Spoon the mixture onto a serving plate. Sprinkle with the lemon juice and parsley and serve warm.

Serves 4

NOTE

When fresh borlotti beans are unavailable, you can make this dish using dried beans. First soak them overnight in plenty of cold water, then drain and cook as directed in the recipe.

FISH & SEAFOOD

When we were kids we used to go fishing with my favourite uncle,
my father and my cousins. The men would catch the fish and
put them in a bucket of water.

My cousin Tulay and I would watch the fish swimming around
in the bucket and we felt sorry for them. Instead of cleaning them,
we would let them go.

The men would exclaim, 'What happened to all the fish?'

We would simply answer, 'They ran away!'

KARİDES GÜVEÇ

YAMBA PRAWN GOULASH

If you have some small ovenproof terracotta pots, you can delight your guests with individual servings. The Australian coastal town of Yamba is famous for its sweet prawns (shrimp) — both its small school prawns, and the medium–large ones we are using here.

60 ml (2 fl oz/¼ cup)
  olive oil
1 onion, diced
3 garlic cloves, chopped
4 long green chillies,
  chopped
2 small green capsicums
  (bell peppers), chopped
500 g (9 oz) tomatoes,
  peeled and chopped
1 kg (2 lb 3 oz) raw Yamba
  prawns (shrimp), peeled
  and deveined, leaving the
  tails intact
15 g (½ oz/½ cup) chopped
  flat-leaf (Italian) parsley,
  plus extra to garnish
30 g (1 oz/½ cup) chopped
  dill
150 g (5½ oz/1 cup)
  crumbled Bulgarian feta

Preheat the oven to 180°C (350°F).

Heat the olive oil in a flameproof casserole dish on the stove top. Add the onion and cook over medium heat for 5 minutes, until soft. Add the garlic and cook for a few minutes more.

Stir in the chilli, capsicum and tomato. Season with sea salt and freshly ground black pepper and cook for another few minutes.

Add the prawns, parsley and dill and cook for a final 2 minutes.

Sprinkle the feta over the mixture, then transfer the dish to the oven and bake for 10 minutes.

Garnish with extra parsley and serve immediately, with crusty bread.

Serves 4–6

SARIMSAKLI İSTAKOZ

GARLIC CHILLI BUGS

Very early one Friday morning, just before a record flood came and stranded everyone, my favourite fisherman, Donald, rang to say he had octopus, crabs, squid and 'jumping bugs' — bugs that were so fresh they were literally jumping! Please don't cringe at this. Everyone enjoyed those magnificent jumping bugs.

Summer is the happiest time for me — we always feast on local squid, prawns (shrimp) and other seafood. I suppose I'll have to give you the recipes for those too.

6 Balmain bugs (see note)
125 ml (4 fl oz/½ cup)
   olive oil
5 garlic cloves, chopped
2 red chillies, diced
15 g (½ oz/½ cup) chopped
   flat-leaf (Italian) parsley
rocket (arugula) leaves, to
   serve (optional)
lemon wedges, to serve

Tomato & onion salad

1 vine-ripened tomato, diced
1 small red onion, diced
80 ml (2½ fl oz/⅓ cup)
   extra virgin olive oil
2–3 tablespoons lemon juice
3 tablespoons finely chopped
   flat-leaf parsley

Place all the tomato and onion salad ingredients in a bowl. Season with sea salt and freshly ground black pepper, then mix together and set aside.

Turn the Balmain bugs upside down on a chopping board. Using a sharp knife, cut the bugs in half lengthways, down the belly. Clean out the guts, then dry the bugs with paper towel.

Heat the olive oil in a large heavy-based frying pan. Add the garlic and chilli and fry over low heat for a few minutes. Add the bugs, then cover and cook for 2–3 minutes.

Turn the bugs over, then cover and cook for a further 2 minutes. Sprinkle with the parsley and some sea salt.

Serve warm, on a bed of rocket leaves if you like, with crusty bread, lemon wedges, and the tomato and onion salad on the side.

Serves 6

NOTE

Balmain bugs, also called butterfly fan lobsters, are a small variety of slipper lobster native to coastal Australia. Langoustine, scampi or small slipper lobsters or crayfish can be used here instead.

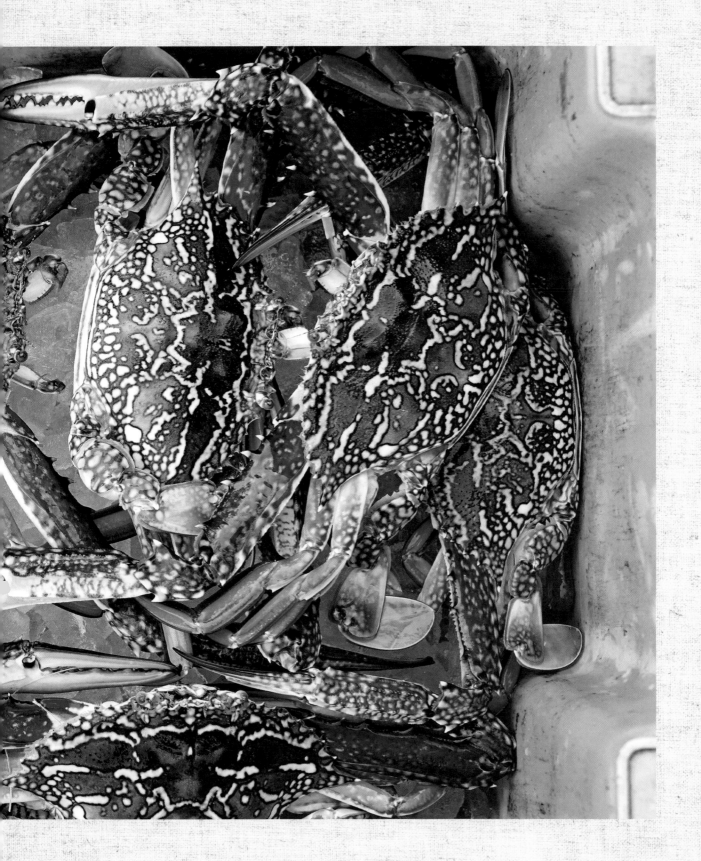

HAMSI KIZARTMASI

FRIED ANCHOVIES

If fresh anchovies are not available, you can use fresh sardines in this recipe. Serve them with the Parsley & red onion salad from page 79, and some lovely crusty bread.

500 g (1 lb 2 oz) fresh
   anchovies
75 g (2¾ oz/½ cup) plain
   (all-purpose) flour
125 ml (4 fl oz/½ cup)
   sunflower oil
lemon wedges, to serve
Parsley & red onion salad
   (page 79), to serve

Gently scrape any scales off the anchovies. To gut them, open the belly using a sharp knife, then scrape out the intestines. Dry the anchovies completely, using paper towel.

Put the flour on a plate or in a bowl and toss the anchovies in the flour. Season with sea salt.

Heat the oil in a deep heavy-based frying pan. When the oil is hot, fry the fish over high heat for about 2 minutes on each side, until crispy.

Serve hot, with the salad and crusty bread.

Serves 4

DOMATESLİ AHTAPOT

BRAISED OCTOPUS IN TOMATO SAUCE

1 kg (2 lb 3 oz) baby
   octopus, cleaned (page 169)
250 ml (8½ fl oz/1 cup)
   white vinegar
250 ml (8½ fl oz/1 cup)
   olive oil
1 onion, diced
2 long green chillies, chopped
6 bay leaves
200 g (7 oz) green olives,
   pitted
1 kg (2 lb 4 oz) tomatoes,
   diced
15 g (½ oz/½ cup) chopped
   flat-leaf (Italian) parsley
lemon wedges, to serve

Place the octopus in a saucepan with the vinegar. Bring to the boil and cook at a boil for about 20 minutes, or until the octopus is gelatinous. Drain and set aside.

Meanwhile, heat the olive oil in a frying pan and fry the onion over medium heat for 5 minutes, or until soft. Add the chilli and cook for 2 minutes, then add the bay leaves, olives, tomato and half the parsley. Cook for a further 10 minutes.

Stir the octopus through the tomato mixture and cook, uncovered, for 5 minutes. Season with sea salt and freshly ground black pepper.

Serve sprinkled with the remaining parsley, with lemon wedges and crusty bread.

The octopus can be braised 3–4 days ahead and gently reheated before serving.

Serves 4–6

ASMA YAPRAKLI SARDALYA

SARDINES WRAPPED IN VINE LEAVES

1 kg (2 lb 3 oz) fresh
   sardines, cleaned and
   gutted
vine leaves, for wrapping the
   sardines
1 garlic clove, chopped
2 bay leaves
sunflower oil, for pan-frying
lemon wedges, to serve

Wash the sardines in fresh water and dry completely using paper towel. Wash the vine leaves and dry them using paper towel.

Sprinkle sea salt and freshly ground black pepper over each sardine, then wrap each fish in its own vine leaf.

Place the garlic, bay leaves and about 2 cm (¾ inch) of oil in a large heavy-based frying pan. Warm the oil over high heat.

When the oil is hot, cook the wrapped sardines, in batches if necessary, for a few minutes on each side.

Serve hot, with lemon wedges.

Serves 4–6

KALAMAR TAVASI

FRIED SQUID

1 kg (2 lb 3 oz) squid,
  cleaned (page 169)
60 g (2 oz/½ cup) cornflour
  (cornstarch)
sunflower oil, for pan-frying
Walnut tarator (page 129),
  to serve

Dry the squid using paper towel, then cut into bite-sized chunks.

In a bowl, mix together the cornflour and a generous pinch of sea salt and freshly ground black pepper.

Heat about 2 cm (¾ inch) of oil in a large heavy-based frying pan over high heat.

In small batches, toss the squid quickly in the cornflour mixture. Fry the squid in small batches for about 4–5 minutes, until just cooked — no longer, or the squid will be tough.

Drain on paper towel and serve immediately, with walnut tarator.

Serves 4–6

AHTAPOT SALATASI

COLD OCTOPUS SALAD

When Donald, my trusty fisherman, brings us bucket-loads of octopus, we quickly put them in the freezer for at least two or three days to tenderise them. This also has the advantage of gently putting them to sleep. Large octopus tentacles also work well in this recipe; you can rub off the skin before serving.

1 kg (2 lb 3 oz) frozen octopus (6–8 small ones)

250 ml (8½ fl oz/1 cup) white vinegar

4 bay leaves

3–4 flat-leaf (Italian) parsley stalks, plus 30 g (1 oz/1 cup) chopped parsley

60 ml (2 fl oz/¼ cup) extra virgin olive oil

60 ml (2 fl oz/¼ cup) lemon juice

3 tablespoons diced red chilli

Defrost the frozen octopus in the refrigerator overnight. Clean the octopus by removing the head and squeezing the beak from the body (see page 169).

Place the octopus in a saucepan with the vinegar, bay leaves, parsley stalks and a good pinch of sea salt. Bring to the boil, then cook at a boil for about 20 minutes, or until the octopus is gelatinous.

Drain the octopus and leave to cool slightly, then chop into bite-sized pieces.

In a bowl, mix together the olive oil, lemon juice, chilli and chopped parsley. Season to taste with sea salt, then toss the octopus through the mixture. Serve cold, or at room temperature.

This salad will keep for 2–3 days in the refrigerator.

Serves 4–6

BARBUNYA TAVASI

FRIED RED MULLET

In Turkey, red mullet is the most beautiful and sought-after little fish. We wrap the fish in vine leaves, we fry them, we just love them. Sometimes Donald brings buckets of sweet local red mullet and puts a big smile on my face. Here is a simple way for you to enjoy them.

If you can't find red mullet, you can also use a sweet white-fleshed fish such as whiting.

1 kg (2 lb 3 oz) red mullet, gutted and cleaned
150 g (5½ oz/1 cup) plain (all-purpose) flour
125 ml (4 fl oz/½ cup) sunflower oil
flat-leaf (Italian) parsley leaves, to serve
rocket (arugula) leaves, to serve
lemon wedges, to serve

Wash the mullet and dry thoroughly using paper towel.

Put the flour in a bowl or on a plate with a little sea salt. Coat the fish in the flour.

Heat the oil in a large frying pan over high heat. When the oil is hot, fry the mullet for 2 minutes on each side, until golden brown and just cooked through.

Serve immediately, on a bed of parsley and rocket leaves, with lemon wedges for squeezing over.

Serves 4–6

MEAT

Red meat in Turkey is quite expensive but loved by all. At home, Turks are most likely to eat more vegetable dishes, or only small amounts of lamb or beef — so when they go out for lunch or dinner, they will order doner kebab or barbecued lamb, because this is more of a treat.

When they do slaughter an animal, Turks consume most parts of it, from head to toe. The brain will become a brain salad. The head will become a soup. The intestines will become part of the sucuk, the Turkish sausage. We even fry and eat the sheep's testicles!

Chickens are also the most beautiful creatures. We roast them, we braise them, we boil them… gosh, we can do so much with them. In Turkey, we barbecue them or bake them with potatoes and tomatoes. In Australia we stuff them — here we go again, you think. But in Turkey we don't stuff them: big surprise!

TAVUK CİĞERİ EZMESİ

CHICKEN LIVER PÂTÉ

This light, scrumptious pâté is not as rich and heavy as French pâté, and is delicious served with pickled cucumbers, black olives and fresh bread. It will keep in the refrigerator for 2–3 days.

80 g (2¾ oz) butter
250 g (9 oz) chicken livers
1 large onion, sliced
5 hard-boiled free-range
  eggs, shelled
extra virgin olive oil, for
  drizzling

Melt the butter in a frying pan. Fry the chicken livers over high heat for 5–6 minutes, or until just cooked but still pink in the middle. Remove from the pan with a slotted spoon and set aside.

Add the onion to the pan and gently fry for 7 minutes, or until soft and lightly golden.

Scrape the onion into a food processor. Add the chicken livers, eggs, sea salt and freshly ground black pepper and blend to a smooth paste.

Transfer to a bowl or plate and serve drizzled with a little olive oil.

Serves 4

ÇERKEZ TAVUGU

CIRCASSIAN CHICKEN WITH PAPRIKA OIL & WALNUT TARATOR

Legend tells us that women of the Circassian region (or the Caucasus as it is known today) were famous for their beauty, and that this exotic dish is named for the pale complexions of the beautiful ladies in the Sultan's harem, luxuriating in magnificent palaces back in the days of the Ottoman Empire.

For the best flavour, please use only the sweetest walnuts and the finest paprika in this simple recipe. This dish is amazing on the first day — and even better the next, served at room temperature as a meze or a main meal. The stock from poaching the chicken can be strained and frozen to be used in a pilaf or stew.

1 small chicken, weighing about 1.4 kg (3 lb 1 oz)
1 onion, chopped
2 carrots, chopped
4 bay leaves

Paprika oil
20 g (¾ oz) butter
60 ml (2 fl oz/¼ cup) olive oil
2 tablespoons sweet paprika

Walnut tarator
20 g (¾ oz/¼ cup) dry breadcrumbs
60 g (2 oz/½ cup) walnuts, crushed
2 garlic cloves, crushed
250 g (9 oz/1 cup) Yoghurt (page 172)

Put all the walnut tarator ingredients in a food processor and blend to a thick paste. Slowly blend in just enough cold water to make a smooth sauce. Season to taste with sea salt. Transfer to a bowl, then cover and allow to rest for a couple of hours.

Meanwhile, wash the chicken in cold water and remove all visible fat.

Place the chicken, onion, carrot and bay leaves in a large saucepan. Season with sea salt and pour in enough water to cover. Bring to the boil, then reduce the heat and gently simmer the chicken for about 1 hour, or until tender and cooked through.

While the chicken is poaching, make the paprika oil. Gently heat the paprika oil ingredients in a small saucepan to melt the butter and warm the oil through, then set aside to infuse.

Once the chicken is cooked, allow it to cool slightly in the poaching liquid, then lift the chicken into a large bowl. Remove and discard all the skin and bones. Shred the meat into bite-sized pieces.

Mix the walnut tarator through the shredded chicken, then place in a serving bowl. Drizzle with the warm paprika oil and serve at room temperature.

Serves 4

NOTE
The tarator can be made up to 12 hours ahead; it will thicken on standing, so thin it with a little water or stock before using it at room temperature.

PİLİÇLİ BAMYA

LEMONY CHICKEN & OKRA

125 ml (4 fl oz/½ cup)
  olive oil
2 onions, diced
500 g (1 lb 2 oz) boneless,
  skinless chicken thighs,
  cut into bite-sized pieces
1 kg (2 lb 3 oz) okra
500 g (1 lb 2 oz) tomatoes,
  diced
2 long green chillies, diced
juice of 1 lemon

Heat the olive oil in a saucepan. Add the onion and gently cook for about 15 minutes, until soft and golden.

Add the chicken to the pan and cook over medium heat for a further 10–15 minutes, stirring occasionally, until the chicken is just cooked through.

Meanwhile, prepare the okra by carefully peeling off the conical tops. If you cut too deeply, it will make the okra slimy.

Add the okra to the pan, along with the tomato and chilli. Season with sea salt and freshly ground black pepper and simmer, uncovered, for a further 20 minutes, until the chicken and okra are tender.

Stir in the lemon juice and serve with crusty bread.

Serves 4

BILDIRGIN TAVASI VE İNGİR YAPRAGI

QUAIL PAN-FRIED ON FIG LEAVES

If you haven't fiddled around butterflying a quail before, ask your butcher, 'Please mister, can you help with this? You're the best butcher in the world.'

The quail in this recipe are pan-fried between layers of fig leaves, but if you don't have any, just cook the quail without them. If you're lucky enough to have some fresh figs, gently break them in half, then throw them into the warm juices in the pan with a generous teaspoon of sugar while the quail is resting. Warm the figs through, serve with the quail and you're in heaven.

4 quail
80 ml (2½ fl oz/⅓ cup)
   olive oil
2 tablespoons pomegranate
   molasses (see note, page 72)
8 fresh fig leaves
Warm lentil salad (page 72),
   to serve

Working with one at a time, place the quail on a chopping board, breast side down. Using a sharp knife or kitchen scissors, cut all the way down along each side of the backbone, to release the backbone. Discard the backbone (or reserve to use when making chicken stock).

Turn the quail over. Using the heel of your palm, firmly press down along the breast bone to flatten the bird. Remove the small sharp rib bones, or work the flesh off the bones with your fingers, to pull the breast cage out.

Rub sea salt into each quail, then massage the olive oil and pomegranate molasses into the skin. Cover and marinate in the refrigerator for at least 2 hours, or overnight.

Place four fig leaves on the bottom of a large non-stick frying pan. Lay the quail on top, then cover them with the remaining fig leaves.

Cover the pan and cook over high heat for 4–5 minutes. Turn the quail over and fry on the other side for a further 4–5 minutes, or until just cooked, being careful not to overcook them.

Remove the pan from the heat and leave covered. Allow the quail to rest for about 5 minutes.

Serve the quail with warm juices from the pan, and warm lentil salad.

Serves 4

ÖRDEK SALATASI

ROAST DUCK SALAD

I cannot cook a chicken or a duck with their bottoms intact. I have to remove these first because I think all the toxins build up in this place. I know some think the 'parson's nose' is delicious, so if you want to keep it and eat it, go for it. The world is your oyster and I won't see it.

1 duck, weighing about
1.5 kg (3 lb 5 oz), tail
removed

1 beetroot (beet), scrubbed
but not peeled

150 g (5½ oz/1 cup)
pumpkin (winter squash),
peeled and cubed

175 g (6 oz/1 cup) fine
burghul (bulgur wheat)

1 small red onion, thinly
sliced

2 red chillies, finely diced

80 ml (2½ fl oz/⅓ cup)
pomegranate molasses
(see note, page 72)

80 ml (2½ fl oz/⅓ cup)
extra virgin olive oil

20 g (¾ oz/1 cup) mint
leaves

30 g (1 oz/1 cup) coriander
(cilantro) leaves

60 g (2 oz/½ cup) Dukkah
(page 170)

Preheat the oven to 200°C (400°F).

Rub sea salt over the duck and place it in a roasting dish, breast side down.

Wrap the beetroot in foil, then place on a non-stick baking tray with the pumpkin. Transfer the duck and vegetables to the oven and bake for 45 minutes, checking the beetroot and pumpkin and removing them from the oven when they are just cooked, and setting them aside to cool.

After the duck has been roasting for 45 minutes, turn it over and bake for a further 45 minutes, or until cooked. (You will know it's cooked if you poke the fattest bit with a skewer and the juice runs clear.) Remove from the oven and allow to cool.

Meanwhile, put the burghul in a small saucepan with 125 ml (4 fl oz/½ cup) water. Bring to the boil, then simmer for 5 minutes, or until just tender. Drain well and set aside.

Rub or peel off the skin from the roasted beetroot. Cut the beetroot into cubes and place in a large bowl with the roasted pumpkin and the burghul. Add the onion, chilli, pomegranate molasses, olive oil, mint, coriander and dukkah. Season to taste with sea salt and freshly ground black pepper, mix together and set aside.

Once the duck has cooled, remove all the skin, then tear or cut the skin into small pieces and set aside. Pull off all the meat, tear into bite-sized pieces and fold the meat through the salad.

Heat a non-stick frying pan over high heat. Fry the duck skin for 5–6 minutes, until nice and crispy.

Sprinkle the crispy duck skin on top of the salad and serve immediately.

Serves 4

PATLICANLI TAVUK

EGGPLANT WITH CHICKEN

250 ml (8½ fl oz/1 cup)
  olive oil
2 eggplants (aubergines), cut
  into 1 cm (½ inch) cubes
1 onion, diced
250 g (9 oz) boneless,
  skinless chicken thighs,
  cut into bite-sized pieces
500 g (1 lb 2 oz) tomatoes,
  diced
1 tablespoon cumin seeds,
  toasted (see note, page 44)
2 long green chillies, diced
15 g (½ oz/½ cup) chopped
  flat-leaf (Italian) parsley

Heat the olive oil in a large frying pan. When the oil is hot, fry the eggplant in batches over high heat for 5–10 minutes, or until soft. Remove with a slotted spoon and set aside.

Fry the onion in the remaining pan oil until soft. Add the chicken and cook over high heat, turning often, for 10 minutes, until browned all over.

Add the tomato, cumin seeds, chilli and parsley. Season with sea salt and freshly ground black pepper and mix well.

Layer the eggplant over the chicken mixture. Cover and cook over low heat for a further 10 minutes.

Serve hot, with yummy bread.

Serves 4

HÜNKAR BEGENDI

SULTAN'S DELIGHT

Turkish people love their eggplant (aubergine), in myriad ways — fried, sautéed, smoked, stuffed, baked. It is said that Turks have over 200 different ways with eggplant. Here is another one, the famous 'Sultan's delight': lamb served on a bed of smoked eggplant cream.

40 g (1½ oz) butter

2 tablespoons olive oil

2 onions, diced

500 g (1 lb 2 oz) boned lamb shoulder, cubed

500 g (1 lb 2 oz) tomatoes, diced

2 long green chillies, chopped

2 garlic cloves, chopped

2 tablespoons tomato paste (concentrated purée)

15 g (½ oz/½ cup) chopped flat-leaf (Italian) parsley

Smoked eggplant cream

1 kg (2 lb 3 oz) charred eggplants (aubergines) (page 169)

juice of 1 lemon

80 g (2¾ oz) butter

35 g (1¼ oz/¼ cup) plain (all-purpose) flour

375 ml (12½ fl oz/1½ cups) warm milk

60 g (2 oz/½ cup) grated cheddar cheese

Heat the butter and olive oil in a heavy-based saucepan. Sauté the onion over medium heat for 5 minutes, or until golden. Increase the heat to high, add the lamb and cook, turning, for 5 minutes, or until browned on all sides.

Stir in the tomato, chilli, garlic, tomato paste and 125 ml (4 fl oz/½ cup) hot water. Bring to the boil, then reduce the heat, cover and simmer for about 1 hour, or until the lamb is tender, adding a little extra water if the mixture becomes dry.

While the lamb is cooking, prepare the eggplant cream. Peel the charred eggplants and place the flesh in a colander. Add the lemon juice and mash the flesh with a fork. Set aside and allow the juices to drain.

Melt the butter in a heavy-based saucepan. Add the flour and cook, stirring, over medium heat, for 2–3 minutes, to make a smooth roux. Add the warm milk and stir until smooth.

Stir in the eggplant, season with sea salt and freshly ground black pepper and cook for a further 5 minutes. Stir in the cheese, remove from the heat and leave to cool.

Spread some eggplant cream over warm serving plates and pile the lamb in the centre. Serve immediately, sprinkled with the parsley.

Serves 4

KUZU KAVURMASI

MY BABA'S LAMB KEBAB

One of my earliest memories of growing up in Turkey is of my Baba making a massive fire and putting our 'sac' over the flames. A sac is a large circular cast-iron pan, like a wok. Usually, women make flatbread on the up-ended curved top of it, but my father turned it upside down. He would pour a little olive oil in it, then add some diced lamb, chopped tomatoes, green chillies and sea salt and freshly ground black pepper. He would stir and stir, while we waited with chunks of bread in our hands. It is the only time we saw our father cook. I was so proud of him. Here is the dish he used to cook for us.

125 ml (4 fl oz/½ cup)
  olive oil
1 large onion, diced
1 kg (2 lb 3 oz) lamb
  backstraps or loin fillets,
  chopped into bite-sized
  pieces
500 g (1 lb 2 oz) tomatoes,
  chopped
250 g (9 oz) green chillies
  (see note), chopped

Heat the oil in a wok, or in a sac if you happen to have one. Add the onion and stir constantly over high heat for a few minutes. Now add the lamb and cook, stirring, for a further 5 minutes.

Add the tomato and chilli and season with sea salt and freshly ground black pepper. Cook, stirring, for a final 5 minutes.

Serve hot, with crusty bread.

Serves 4–6

NOTE

Turkish chillies are typically long, pale green chillies (known in Turkey as biber, or pepper). They are usually sweet, but can also be hot. Turks love them for breakfast, lunch and dinner. If you can't find Turkish biber, just use long green chillies.

PATATES OTURTMASI

POTATOES WITH LAMB, TOMATOES & GREEN CHILLI

If you happen to have any leftovers when you make this dish, don't worry — it keeps well in the refrigerator and will still be highly delicious a few days later.

1 kg (2 lb 3 oz) tomatoes

250 ml (8½ fl oz/1 cup) olive oil

1 large onion, diced

2 tablespoons tomato paste (concentrated purée)

500 g (1 lb 2 oz) minced (ground) lamb

3 long green chillies, diced

15 g (½ oz/½ cup) chopped flat-leaf (Italian) parsley, plus extra to garnish

1 kg (2 lb 3 oz) desiree or other all-purpose potatoes, peeled and cut into slices 5 mm (¼ inch) thick

Cucumber yoghurt (page 14), to serve

Dice half the tomatoes and set aside. Slice the remaining tomatoes and set aside separately.

Heat the olive oil in a saucepan, then gently fry the onion until soft and golden. Stir in the diced tomato, the tomato paste, lamb and chilli. Season with sea salt and freshly ground black pepper and cook, stirring, for 5 minutes. Stir in the parsley and set aside.

Arrange a single layer of the potato slices in a large saucepan. Spoon one-quarter of the lamb mixture over the potato, then a layer of the sliced tomatoes. Sprinkle with sea salt.

Now add another layer of the potato, then the lamb mixture, then the sliced tomatoes and a sprinkling of sea salt. Continue layering until all the ingredients are used, finishing with a layer of sliced tomatoes.

Pour 250 ml (8½ fl oz/1 cup) water over the top, then cover with a lid or foil. Gently simmer for 30–45 minutes, until the potato is tender and the lamb is cooked.

Garnish with extra parsley and serve hot, with some cucumber yoghurt on the side.

Serves 6–8

KUZU VE AYVA YAHNISI

LAMB SHANKS WITH QUINCE

Quinces smell delicious. When we were kids we would tap them on a rock to bruise them, then slice them — they tasted like heaven. My mum used to make quince jam; sometimes she would also bake quince with a little sugar and a little water. The quince would turn the most amazing ruby-red colour and she would serve it with yoghurt and pistachio nuts for breakfast. Imagine waking up to that! You can also stuff quince with lamb, or bake them with lamb shanks in the oven, as we do here. So many options.

60 ml (2 fl oz/¼ cup)
   vegetable oil
4 lamb shanks
2 tablespoons plain
   (all-purpose) flour
40 g (1½ oz) butter
2 tablespoons sugar
155 g (5½ oz/1 cup)
   chopped onion
3 garlic cloves, chopped
2 cinnamon sticks
½ teaspoon ground allspice
2 tablespoons lemon juice
4 small quinces
chopped flat-leaf (Italian)
   parsley, to garnish

Heat the oil in a large heavy-based saucepan or flameproof casserole dish over high heat.

Toss the lamb shanks in the flour with a pinch of sea salt, shaking off the excess flour. Brown the shanks in the pan for 10 minutes, turning constantly. Remove the shanks and set aside.

Carefully drain the oil from the pan and discard.

Wipe the pan clean and place back over the heat. Add the butter, sugar, onion, garlic, cinnamon and allspice. Add a generous sprinkling of sea salt and freshly ground black pepper and mix to combine. Pour in 250 ml (8½ fl oz/1 cup) water, then put the shanks back in.

Cover the pan and bring to the boil, then reduce the heat and leave the shanks to simmer for 1½ hours.

Meanwhile, add the lemon juice to a large bowl of water. Working with one at a time, peel each quince, cut into quarters and remove the core, adding the quince quarters to the bowl of lemon water as you work, so they don't turn brown.

Add the quince to the lamb, then cover and cook for a further 1 hour, or until the meat is tender and the quince is soft.

Garnish with parsley and serve hot, with Turkish bread.

Serves 4

IZGARA PİRZOLA

LAMB CUTLETS

4 lamb cutlets
2 tablespoons dried oregano
125 ml (4 fl oz/½ cup)
  olive oil

Flatten the cutlets using a meat tenderiser, rolling pin or a bottle of wine.

Place the cutlets in a container and sprinkle with the oregano. Pour the olive oil over and turn the cutlets to coat them in the oil. Cover and marinate in the refrigerator for at least 8 hours.

Scrape the oregano off the cutlets and sprinkle them with sea salt and freshly ground black pepper.

Cook the cutlets in a hot frying pan or on a hot barbecue for 3–4 minutes on each side for medium-rare cutlets.

Remove from the heat, leave to rest in a warm place for a few minutes, then serve immediately.

Serves 4

LAHMACUN

LAMB PIDE

Here's a recipe for a classic Turkish 'pizza', loved the world over. If you have any dough left over after baking the pide, heat the baking tray in the oven again until very hot. Roll the dough into 20 cm (8 inch) circles and bake them in the oven for 5 minutes, to make little pocket breads.

If you are lucky enough to have a wood-fired oven, you can stretch the dough out thinly and make lavash bread, as well as your pides.

You can also cook the pide in a pizza oven. Heat the pizza oven until hot. Roll each ball of dough into thin sheets, spread a thin layer of topping over each and bake until golden brown.

2 tablespoons olive oil

1 onion, finely diced

250 g (9 oz) minced (ground) lamb

30 g (1 oz/1 cup) chopped flat-leaf (Italian) parsley, plus extra to garnish

2 long green chillies, finely diced

2 tomatoes, finely diced

2 tablespoons tomato paste (concentrated purée)

lemon wedges, to serve

Dough

½ teaspoon sugar

1 teaspoon dried yeast

450 g (1 lb/3 cups) plain (all-purpose) flour

80 ml (2½ fl oz/⅓ cup) olive oil

To make the dough, mix the sugar and yeast in a large bowl with 300 ml (10 fl oz) lukewarm water. Allow the yeast to activate for a few minutes.

Add the flour and a pinch of sea salt and mix into a dough, using your hands. Knead in the bowl until the dough feels like your earlobe. Cover and leave to rise in a warm place for 1 hour.

Punch the dough down and knead in the bowl for another 5 minutes. Cover and leave to rise for a further 1 hour.

Roll the ball of dough in the olive oil. Cover and leave to rest for a further 1 hour, until doubled in size.

Meanwhile, make the topping. Heat the olive oil in a frying pan and gently fry the onion until golden. Add the remaining topping ingredients, except the lemon wedges. Season with sea salt and freshly ground black pepper and stir together for a few minutes, ensuring all the ingredients are well mixed. The lamb should remain partially uncooked, as you will be baking it in the oven.

Place the topping mixture in a strainer and set aside to drain.

Preheat the oven to 200°C (400°F). Heat two large baking trays in the oven until very hot.

Punch the dough down again and divide into 12 small balls. Let the dough rest again for 2–3 minutes, then roll each ball out to a 20 cm (8 inch) circle. Spread each one with about 2 tablespoons of the topping and place on the hot baking trays (you may need to work in batches).

Bake for 10 minutes, or until the bread is is golden.

Garnish with extra parsley and serve hot, with lemon wedges.

Serves 12

SWEETS

When we were children, Baba would give us spending money.
I would spend all my money on chocolate bars. My sister would
hide hers, then send me to the corner store to buy her Turkish
delight and biscuits (cookies). Her favourites were hazelnut and
coconut Turkish delight and plain sweet biscuits. She would put
the Turkish delight between two biscuits and then squeeze, making
tiny curls of delight through the holes. Her face would light up
like a shining moon.

Traditionally, we do not have dessert with meze. Usually we
eat fresh slices of watermelon, honeydew or rockmelon. However,
for those with a sweet tooth who need something after a few
tipples, here are some indulgences.

FRAMBOAZLI TATLI

MASCARPONE WITH RASPBERRY & BOYSENBERRY TORTE

Even though this is not quite the traditional way with meze, all my lovely guests insist on this recipe. So here you have it — I hope you are happy now!

200 g (7 oz) packet savoiardi
   (lady fingers/sponge finger
   biscuits)
500 ml (17 fl oz/2 cups)
   thickened (whipping)
   cream
230 g (8 oz/1 cup) caster
   (superfine) sugar
250 g (9 oz) mascarpone
250 g (9 oz/1 cup) Yoghurt
   (page 172)
125 g (4½ oz/1 cup)
   raspberries
125 g (4½ oz/1 cup)
   boysenberries

Cover the base of a large springform cake tin with one layer of biscuits (see note below).

In a large bowl, beat the cream, sugar and mascarpone until quite firm, using an electric mixer. Fold the yoghurt through the mixture.

Spread half the mascarpone mixture over the biscuits. Sprinkle the berries over the top.

Spoon the remaining mascarpone mixture over the berries, then cover and refrigerate for at least 3–4 hours.

Cut into wedges and serve.

Generously serves 10

NOTE

You can also make this torte in a glass bowl for decorative effect. Start with a layer of biscuits, then alternate the mascarpone mixture, berries and more biscuits over the top, finishing with a layer of berries.

MUHALLEBİ

MILK PUDDINGS

Serve these delightful puddings sprinkled with crushed pistachio nuts, or with stuffed figs or caramelised figs — whatever your heart chooses.

45 g (1½ oz/¼ cup) rice
   flour
2 tablespoons cornflour
   (cornstarch)
55 g (2 oz/¼ cup) sugar
1 litre (34 fl oz/4 cups) milk
150 g (5½ oz/½ cup)
   pistachio nuts
1 vanilla bean

Combine the rice flour, cornflour, sugar, milk and pistachios in a saucepan. Using a small sharp knife, slice the vanilla bean in half lengthways. Scrape the vanilla seeds into the milk mixture, then drop the bean pod in as well. Mix together well.

Stirring constantly, cook over high heat for 10–15 minutes, or until the mixture thickens enough to thickly coat the back of the spoon. Remove the vanilla bean pod.

Pour into six individual 250 ml (8½ fl oz/1 cup) serving dishes. Cover and refrigerate for a few hours, until chilled.

Serves 6

LOKMA TATLISI

LITTLE DUMPLINGS

I remember my Mama frying up these golden nuggets when I was a little girl. I would get so excited, I just loved them so very much. And I love them still.

300 g (10½ oz/2 cups) plain
(all-purpose) flour
2 tablespoons sugar
1 tablespoon baking powder
3 free-range eggs
250 g (9 oz/1 cup) Yoghurt
(page 172)
sunflower oil, for pan-frying
1 quantity Sugar syrup
(page 172)

In a bowl, mix together the flour, sugar, baking powder, eggs and yoghurt.
Heat about 5 cm (2 inches) of oil in a saucepan over high heat.
When the oil is hot, drop teaspoonfuls of the batter into the pan and fry for 5–8 minutes, turning occasionally, until golden brown all over.
Drain the dumplings and toss them in the cooled sugar syrup.
They are delicious warm or cold.

Serves 6

BEYAZ PEYNIR VE KARPUZ

WATERMELON & FETA

500 g (1 lb 2 oz) portion
  of juicy watermelon
  (about ¼ of a melon)
200 g (7 oz) Bulgarian feta

Carefully remove the thick green skin and white rind from the melon.
  Cut the watermelon flesh into bite-sized pieces, and also cut the
feta into bite-sized pieces. Arrange the watermelon and feta on a large
serving platter.
  Take a bite of your watermelon, a chunk of your feta and a sip of raki.
The world is a beautiful place!

Serves 4

VİŞNELİ VE BADEMLI KEK

CHERRY & ALMOND CAKE

Instead of roasting the almonds in this recipe, you could use the same quantity of almond meal. Lightly toast the almond meal in a dry frying pan before adding it to the cake.

250 g (9 oz) almonds

140 g (5 oz) unsalted butter

230 g (8 oz/1 cup) caster (superfine) sugar

6 free-range eggs

175 g (6 oz/1 cup) rice flour

1 tablespoon baking powder

zest of 3 oranges, shredded or chopped

250 g (9 oz/2¼ cups) pitted sour cherries (see note)

Preheat the oven to 180°C (350°F). Butter and flour a 27 cm (11 inch) springform cake tin.

Spread the almonds on a baking tray and roast for 15–20 minutes, or until lightly browned. Transfer to a food processor and blitz until finely ground. Tip into a bowl and set aside.

Add the butter and sugar to the food processor, then blend together for a few minutes. Add the eggs, one at a time. Now add the rice flour, baking powder, ground almonds and orange zest all at once and mix them through.

Spoon the mixture into the cake tin. Arrange the cherries on top, and around the edges, so that when people cut into the cake, everyone will get pieces of little cherries and there will be nothing left on the plate.

Bake for 40 minutes, or until a skewer inserted into the middle of the cake comes out clean. Leave to cool before removing from the tin.

Serve the cake at room temperature. It will keep for 3–4 days in an airtight container out of the refrigerator.

Serves 8–10

NOTE

Sour cherries are loved throughout Turkey, and add a luscious tang to this cake. If you can't find any, just use regular pitted cherries.

ŞEKERPARE

ALMOND CAKES IN SUGAR SYRUP

These are perfect whenever you feel like a sweet little temptation. They will keep for up to 1 week in an airtight container and are luscious served with fresh cream or yoghurt.

115 g (4 oz/½ cup) caster
　(superfine) sugar
120 g (4½ oz) butter
1 free-range egg, beaten,
　plus 1 beaten egg yolk,
　for brushing
300 g (10½ oz/2 cups)
　self-raising flour
zest of 2 oranges, finely
　chopped
2 tablespoons semolina
80 g (2¾ oz/½ cup)
　blanched almonds
1 quantity Sugar syrup
　(page 172)

Preheat the oven to 200°C (400°F). Oil a large baking tray.

In a large bowl, beat the sugar and butter together using an electric mixer until creamy. Add the beaten whole egg, the flour, orange zest, semolina and a pinch of sea salt.

Using your hands, knead the mixture in the bowl, or on a bench, until it forms a smooth paste.

Break off walnut-sized pieces of the dough and place on the baking tray, leaving a little space in between. Slightly flatten each one, then place an almond in the centre of each. Brush with the beaten egg yolk.

Bake for 25–30 minutes, or until the cakes are cooked through and golden brown.

Remove from the oven. While the cakes are still hot, pour the cooled sugar syrup over.

Serve at room temperature.

Serves 8

CEVİZLİ INCIR PASTASI

FIG & WALNUT CAKE

Hey sisters and brothers, you're going to love this one! This cake keeps well in the refrigerator for up to a week, and is delicious both warm and cold. Try it toasted for breakfast, topped with fresh ricotta.

5 fresh figs, roughly chopped

2 tablespoons semolina

400 g (14 oz/1¾ cups) caster
   (superfine) sugar

3 free-range eggs

zest of 3 oranges, shredded
   or chopped

125 ml (4 fl oz/½ cup)
   olive oil

125 g (4½ oz/½ cup) melted
   butter

250 g (9 oz/1 cup) Yoghurt
   (page 172)

300 g (10½ oz/2 cups)
   self-raising flour

125 g (4½ oz/1 cup)
   walnuts, chopped

Preheat the oven to 180°C (350°F). Butter and flour a 27 cm (11 inch) springform cake tin.

Mix the figs and semolina together with 3 tablespoons of the caster sugar. Set aside.

Put the remaining caster sugar in a bowl with the eggs. Beat using an electric mixer until pale. Add the orange zest, olive oil, butter and yoghurt and mix together. Fold the flour and walnuts through the mixture.

Spoon half the batter into the cake tin, then scatter the fig mixture evenly over the top. Spoon the remaining batter over.

Bake for 40 minutes, or until a skewer inserted into the middle of the cake comes out clean. You'll know your cake is cooked!

Leave to cool before removing from the tin.

Serves 8–10

DUTLU VE GÜLLÜ KEK

MULBERRY & ROSE PETAL CAKE

Most of the mulberries I have seen in Turkey are white. The only place I've ever seen a red mulberry tree is at the sacred site of the tomb of Haci Bektasi Veli, in the town of Kirsehir. My family are of the Alevi faith, a religious minority with our own spiritual practices and culture, and Haci Bektasi Veli is one of our spiritual leaders with his beautiful poems and his philosophy. We love him and respect his wisdom.

So years later, when I came to Australia, I saw these beautiful red and purple juicy babies and fell in love with them. If you cannot find mulberries, you can substitute boysenberries. Haci Bektasi Veli may not be impressed, but he will understand — he is a most forgiving man!

This is my cake for him, and for you.

150 g (5½ oz) butter

345 g (12 oz/1½ cups) caster (superfine) sugar

3 free-range eggs

125 g (4½ oz/½ cup) Yoghurt (page 172)

300 g (10½ oz/2 cups) self-raising flour

125 ml (4 fl oz/½ cup) olive oil

15 g (½ oz/1 cup) unsprayed red rose petals (or use dried ones from a Middle Eastern grocery store)

250 g (9 oz) mulberries

Preheat the oven to 180°C (350°F). Butter and flour a 27 cm (11 inch) springform cake tin.

In a food processor, blend the butter and sugar together for a few minutes. Add the eggs, one at a time. Briefly mix the yoghurt through, then the flour, then the olive oil, being careful not to overwork the gluten in the flour. Add the rose petals and pulse for a few seconds.

Spoon half the batter into the cake tin. Arrange the mulberries evenly on top of the batter. Spoon the remaining batter over the top.

Bake for 40 minutes, or until a skewer inserted into the middle of the cake comes out clean. Leave to cool before removing from the tin.

This cake is delicious served warm or cold. It will keep for 2–3 days in an airtight container in the refrigerator.

Serves 8–10

BASICS

This little chapter explains a few basic techniques for preparing
some common vegetable and seafood ingredients used in Turkish
cuisine. It also includes a handful of simple but versatile
base recipes that feature in several other dishes in this book.
Don't worry, they are all very easy to do.

Soon you'll be cooking like a meze superstar!

TECHNIQUES

PREPARING ARTICHOKE HEARTS

Artichokes are abundant in Turkey. At every local market you will find artichoke hearts sitting in little bowls of water with lemon juice. While fresh whole artichokes are readily available here in season, the prepared hearts are not as easy to find, so here's what you do.

2 lemons
globe artichokes

Add the juice from one lemon to a bowl of cold water; the lemon juice will stop the artichokes browning once they've been cut. Slice the other lemon and have it close by.

Wash the artichokes well, then cut the stems off, near the base. Rub each cut surface with a lemon slice as you work, to prevent discolouring.

Remove the outer three or four layers of leaves, to get to the tender inner leaves. Trim off about 3 cm (1¼ inch) from the top and rub with lemon slices.

Scoop out the hairy inner chokes and any thorny leaves from the centre, using a spoon or melon ball scoop. Place each artichoke heart in the lemon water as soon as you have finished trimming each one.

Cook as soon as possible after preparation, as recipes direct.

CHARRING EGGPLANT

Poke four or five holes in each eggplant, using a sharp knife. Place the eggplant directly over the burner on a gas stove, or on a barbecue grill over high heat. Turning the eggplant constantly with tongs, cook for about 10 minutes, or until the neck of the eggplant is soft.

Set the eggplant aside until cool enough to handle, then peel off and discard the skin. Place the eggplant in a strainer and let the bitter juices drain for about 10 minutes.

Use as required in other recipes.

CLEANING OCTOPUS

Using a small knife, carefully cut between the head and tentacles of the octopus, just below the eyes. Grasp the body of the octopus and push the beak out and up through the centre of the tentacles with your finger. Cut the eyes from the head of the octopus by slicing a small disc off with a sharp knife. Discard the eye section. To clean the octopus head, carefully slit through one side, avoiding the ink sac, and scrape out any gut from inside. Rinse under running water to remove any remaining grit.

CLEANING SQUID

To clean squid, gently pull the tentacles away from the tube (the intestines should come away at the same time). Remove the intestines from the tentacles by cutting under the eyes, then remove the beak if it remains in the centre of the tentacles by using your fingers to push up the centre.

Pull away the quill (the transparent cartilage) from inside the body and discard. Remove and discard any white membrane. Under cold running water, pull away the skin from the hood.

RECIPES

DUKKAH

Dukkah is delicious for dipping bread into and for sprinkling over other dishes. For a simply superb treat, put some good olive oil in a small dipping bowl, some pomegranate molasses in another, and some dukkah in a third, then dip some good Turkish bread into all three.

150 g (5½ oz) hazelnuts
60 g (2 oz) coriander seeds
  (about 10 tablespoons)
50 g (1¾ oz) cumin seeds
  (about 5 tablespoons)
100 g (3½ oz/⅔ cup)
  sesame seeds
1 teaspoon sea salt
½ teaspoon freshly ground
  black pepper

Preheat the oven to 200°C (400°F). Spread the hazelnuts on a baking tray and roast for 10 minutes, or until the skins have started to crack, keeping careful watch that they don't burn.

Remove from the oven and allow to cool slightly, then tip the hazelnuts into a sieve and shake the skins loose, or tip them into a clean cloth and rub the skins off.

Roughly chop the hazelnuts in a food processor, then transfer to a small bowl and set aside.

Place a small non-stick frying pan over medium heat, without any oil. Add the coriander seeds and toast for 3–5 minutes, or until fragrant, tossing regularly so they don't burn. Remove from the pan and roughly grind, using a mortar and pestle or a spice grinder. Add to the ground hazelnuts.

Toast the cumin seeds in the same frying pan for about 2 minutes, until fragrant, tossing so they don't burn. Roughly grind using the mortar and pestle or spice grinder, then add to the hazelnut mixture.

Lastly, toast the sesame seeds in the frying pan for 2–3 minutes, until lightly browned and fragrant, ensuring they don't burn. Add them to the hazelnut mixture, along with the salt and pepper.

Fold all the ingredients together. Transfer to a sealed jar and keep in the refrigerator or in a cool, dark place.

Makes about 375 g (13 oz)

İÇ PİLAV

RICE PILAF

Once you have prepared this basic pilaf and used it to stuff 'whatever it is your heart has desired', any leftovers can be kept in the refrigerator for 3–4 days. The pilaf can also be frozen for use in emergencies.

125 ml (4 fl oz/½ cup)
  olive oil
1 large onion, diced
40 g (1½ oz/¼ cup) pine
  nuts
400 g (14 oz/2 cups)
  long-grain white rice
35 g (1¼ oz/¼ cup) currants
2 tablespoons tomato paste
  (concentrated purée)
½ teaspoon sugar
2 tablespoons water,
  approximately
30 g (1 oz/½ cup) chopped
  dill
15 g (½ oz/½ cup) chopped
  flat-leaf (Italian) parsley
2 tablespoons dried mint

Heat the olive oil in a saucepan and gently fry the onion until golden. Add the pine nuts and brown them for few minutes, stirring often.

Stir in the rice, currants, tomato paste and sugar and season with sea salt and freshly ground black pepper. Add some of the water and cook slowly for 10 minutes, or until the rice is slightly nutty in texture — you want the rice to remain a little undercooked; only add more water if needed to prevent the rice sticking to the pan.

Remove from the heat and allow the mixture to cool slightly. Stir in the herbs, then use as required in other recipes.

Makes about 1.35 kg (3 lb)

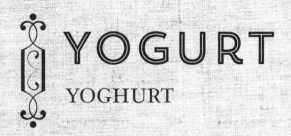

YOGURT

YOGHURT

In Turkey, yoghurt is consumed at a higher rate than in probably any other country. It is made into dips, enjoyed in dishes savoury and sweet — in just about any way you can possibly imagine. And, of course, it is the best yoghurt in the world! It is thick and creamy and has been made for centuries by mothers, grandmothers, great-grandmothers and their mothers. We eat it, we drink it, we put it on our faces (for beauty, of course). Nothing can be done without yoghurt.

2 litres (68 fl oz/8 cups)
  milk
90 g (3¼ oz/⅓ cup) plain
  unsweetened yoghurt —
  preferably a good organic
  one, with lots of healthy
  live cultures

Heat the milk in a large saucepan to 85°C (185°F), or until you can put your little finger in and hold it there for a few seconds. Remove from the heat and allow to cool to 45°C (115°F).

Place the yoghurt in a bowl and mix in 250 ml (8½ fl oz/1 cup) of the warm milk. Return this mixture to the milk in the pan and mix well.

Cover with a lid, then wrap the pan in a blanket and place in a warm spot for 8 hours. Voilà — you now have your very own yoghurt.

Remove the blanket and place the pan in the refrigerator to cool for 3 hours. Do not stir as it will disturb the yoghurt.

The yoghurt will keep in the refrigerator for up to 2 weeks.

Makes about 2 kg (4½ lb/8 cups)

SUGAR SYRUP

440 g (15½ oz/2 cups) sugar
2 tablespoons lemon juice

Put the sugar and lemon juice in a saucepan with 250 ml (8½ fl oz/ 1 cup) water. Bring to the boil, stir well and cook over medium heat for 10–15 minutes, until the sugar has dissolved and the liquid has reduced.

Set aside and allow to cool. Transfer to an airtight container and keep in the refrigerator for up to 1 week.

Makes about 375 ml (13 fl oz/1½ cups)

SÜZME

YOGHURT CHEESE

Süzme is also called 'labneh' in other Middle Eastern countries. To make it we put some yoghurt in a sheet of muslin (cheesecloth) and drain off all the liquid, until the yoghurt is thick and almost the texture of cream cheese.

It tastes divine, with all the tangy juices of the yoghurt gone. Now it can be spread on toast with honey and tahini, and eaten for breakfast or dessert. It is absolutely amazing and you will love this, even if you have never loved yoghurt before.

When I was a little girl I would take a spoonful of süzme and spread it on flatbread with a tablespoon of sugar. I would then cover it with another piece of flatbread and wait with great anticipation until my bread became soggy and the sugar dissolved. That was heaven! But it is also delicious in meze.

1 kg (2 lb 3 oz/4 cups)
   Yoghurt (page 172)

Line a strainer with a piece of muslin (cheesecloth). Suspend the strainer over a large bowl, then pour the yoghurt in. Twist the muslin around the top and place a heavy plate on top. Leave the yoghurt to drain in the refrigerator for about 8 hours.

(When I was growing up we would tie the bag of muslin to the washing line, but I don't know how suitable this technique will be for your particular climate. If it suits you, you can try hanging it on your washing line, sisters or brothers!)

Now you have süzme and you can use it in my other delicious recipes.

The süzme will keep in the refrigerator for 2–3 weeks.

Makes about 500 g (1 lb 2 oz/2 cups)

INDEX

ACKNOWLEDGMENTS

First of all, I would like to thank my darling mother. It has been her dream to visit Australia and see where I live, and though it has taken her 28 years to get here, her timing couldn't be any more amazing. She has worked so hard to support this book and I love her to bits.

Thank you to Gwenyth Pegler for being there for me over the years. I love you bucketloads!

To Sally Abrahams, for being the best secretary general going around.

To Paul and Anne Commerford; Syd Mattock; Don, Lyn, Karl and Jess Causley; Glenn and Catherine Porter; and Bob Kershaw, for letting us use their beautiful gardens and farms.

To all my suppliers for bringing me the freshest and best produce over the years.

To Belinda Sanders for being a great personal stylist.

To all of the women from Angourie, Wooloweyah and Yamba, thank you for spoiling my mum and making her feel at home. You know who you are, and that I love you all!

To the staff of the Beachwood Cafe, for being simply wonderful.

To the supermodels who feature throughout this book, thank you for getting out of bed for less than $10,000.

To everyone who helped bring this book into existence, thank you for all of your hard work: Fiona Hardie and Sandy Grant, Paul McNally, Heather Menzies, Alicia Taylor, Sarah DeNardi, Tania Gomes, Katri Hilden, Caroline Jones, Rihana Ries, Michael Hart and Emilia Pettinato.

And last, but not least, to all the people who have visited the Beachwood Cafe in Yamba and Angourie. You walked through the door of my cafe and into my heart.

An SBS Book

Published in 2013 by Hardie Grant Books

Hardie Grant Books (Australia)
Ground Floor, Building 1
658 Church Street
Richmond, Victoria 3121
www.hardiegrant.com.au

Hardie Grant Books (UK)
Dudley House, North Suite
34–35 Southampton Street
London WC2E 7HF
www.hardiegrant.co.uk

A Cataloguing-in-Publication entry is available from the catalogue of the National
Library of Australia at www.nla.gov.au

Turkish Meze
978 1 74270 665 8

Publishing Director: Paul McNally
Project Editor: Rihana Ries
Editor: Katri Hilden
Design Manager: Heather Menzies
Designer: Tania Gomes
Typesetter: Megan Ellis
Photographer: Alicia Taylor *(excluding 70, 90, 150, 166)*
Stylist: Sarah DeNardi
Recipe Tester: Caroline Jones
Production Manager: Todd Rechner

Colour reproduction by Splitting Image Colour Studio
Printed and bound in China by 1010 Printing International Limited